Evaluating Training

The Competent Trainer's Toolkit Series
by David G. Reay

Evaluating Training is the final 'tool' in the series. The first — *Understanding the Training Function* — stands outside the training cycle. The rest, including this book, deal with the cycle stage by stage, from planning your initial strategy right through to evaluating the contribution training makes to the prosperity of your organization.

All these books can be used on training courses or as aids to self-development.

Evaluating Training

DAVID G REAY

Kogan Page Ltd, London
Nichols Publishing Company,
New Jersey

Published in association with **OTSU** LIMITED

First published in 1994

Kogan Page Limited
120 Pentonville Road
London N1 9JN

© OTSU Ltd 1994

Published in the United States of America by Nichols Publishing,
PO Box 6036, East Brunswick, New Jersey 08816

British Library Cataloguing in Publication Data

A CIP record of this book is available from the British Library.
ISBN: (UK) 0 7494 1288 7
ISBN: (US) 0-89397-426-9

Printed and bound in Great Britain by Biddles Ltd, Guildford and King's Lynn

Contents

Acknowledgements

This series is to a large extent based on OTSU's experiences during the past decade. Because of this, so many people have been involved in its formulation, it would be impossible to name them all. However, there are a number of people without whose help this series would not have seen the light of day.

I would like therefore to give my sincere thanks to Paul Leach for his constant support with writing, Adrian Spooner for his editing skill, Aidan Lynn for setting the series in motion, Jill Sharpe and Kathleen Gibson for design and desk-top publishing, Dorothy Reay and Amanda Froggatt for proof-reading and finally Dolores Black at Kogan Page who didn't mind flexible deadlines.

Introduction

Who this book is for

The audience I had in mind as I wrote this book was trainers and training managers who are evaluating or are about to evaluate their training provision. However, I hope this book will serve the needs of a wider audience. Effective evaluation is, in my experience, a never ending process carried out by the training function, and one which can involve line managers, supervisors and trainees in a whole range of evaluation assignments. Any or all of these people could usefully dip into this book.

The other group of people with a vested interest in the evaluation of training is the group who purchase the training. These people, too, may find it helpful to become better informed about what is involved in evaluating training, because it's the evaluation process which tells them whether of not they're getting value for money.

Effective evaluation **is** crucial. For too long evaluation has been seen in some quarters as an appendage — something you can do if there's time; other organizations have banished evaluation to the realms of pure instinct: 'if it feels right, carry on doing it' seems to be the watchword. Even where evaluation is practised, it is too often regarded as a tool to be applied after training is complete — and not as something which may also be used to help you plan and monitor your training throughout the stages of development and implementation.

One thing this book is not, is an academic treatise on evaluation. Others have already produced excellent textbooks of a more academic nature. This book is about the application of evaluation processes which can be used by an active training department, and I've included a range of techniques you might use, but as you might expect, there are others. If you want to take things further, I suggest you read books from the recommended reading section.

Objectives

By the time you've worked through this book, you will be better able to:

- explain the meanings of the terms evaluation, summative evaluation and formative evaluation

- describe those aspects of an organization to which evaluation can make a measurable contribution

- apply various evaluation techniques at key stages in your training development and implementation

- explain the importance of learning objectives to the evaluation process

- select the methods of evaluation most relevant to specific circumstances

- recognize the point at which the training cycle is complete and a new training cycle should start.

Overview

To help you find your way round this book I have prepared an overview so that you can see what is contained in each chapter.

Chapter 1 — Reasons for Evaluation

In this chapter you'll explore just what it is that evaluation can achieve — indeed, needs to achieve if training is to contribute effectively to the organization's prosperity. You'll see that there are six separate targets, all of them worthwhile, within the scope of an effective evaluation.

Chapter 2 — Features of an Evaluation

Here you will see that an evaluation needs to be both valid and reliable. You'll look at these terms in some detail so that, by the end of the chapter, you will be able to take the main points and apply them to your current or planned evaluation techniques.

Chapter 3 — Evaluating the Training Function

Throughout this book the role which evaluation can play in the formation and design of training is stressed, and in this chapter you'll look at the points in the training cycle at which you will find it useful to evaluate. These points are not limited to your current training provision: there are aspects of your strategic planning, your needs analyses and your training selection techniques — to name but three areas — which all deserve scrutiny. If this all sounds like extra work, don't worry. You'll see how a lot of evaluation happens automatically: you could be evaluating already without actually knowing it.

Chapter 4 — Evaluating Your Training

Here you can identify the three points in your current training at which evaluation is appropriate, and study in some detail the benefits of continuous evaluation.

Chapter 5 — Evaluative Techniques

Now that you've seen where and when you need to evaluate, you are ready to look at the different techniques which may be appropriate in the different circumstances. The techniques range from the informal to the strictly formal, and you'll see how there is a place in your repertoire for all types of evaluation.

Chapter 6 — Reacting to Evaluation

An evaluation is not an end in itself. You can't just close the lid on a piece of training and move on to the next simply because you've evaluated it. Evaluation will always throw up questions and challenges. In this chapter you'll see what those questions and challenges might be, and ways of reacting to them.

How to Use This Book

This is not a text which you will read once and then put away never to read again (I hope!). Its inclusion in the *Competent Trainer's Toolkit* indicates that it is for you to use in your work as a trainer.

How you work though the book is really up to you. You may, if you wish, work through the pages in order from front to back and cover the whole text in that way. The book is constructed logically so that you can work right through it. Alternatively, you can dip into it a chapter at a time, as and when you need to.

There is a range of assignments and activities for you to complete throughout the text. Activities are distinguished by the fact that there is some feedback — not always in the form of right or wrong answers, because there are not always right or wrong answers to be had.

Assignments, on the other hand, are an opportunity for you to get out into your organization and ask some of the questions which will enable you to analyse your own situation and evaluate your own training provision. It would be misleading of me to include any answers, although I have included comments from my own organization's experiences with a variety of clients where appropriate. However, when reading these you should bear in mind that your own situation is bound to have its unique features.

As an additional benefit, working through the assignments in the book will enable you to create a body of evidence for your vocational qualification. You should keep this text and the outcomes of the assignments as a record of your study.

Because this book calls on you to write your own thoughts and think about your own situation, it will become your own personal record and guide to evaluation and all it means for the success of your training function and your organization.

Training and Development Lead Body Competences

Many trainers and training managers in the UK are actively seeking professional vocational qualifications, through the National Vocational Qualification route. There are competences at level 3 and 4 of the NVQ in Training and Development for which you will be able to use this book as part of your portfolio of evidence.

I have prepared, on the following page, a matrix which matches a list of assignments in this book and the competences, published in autumn 1994, which appear in the scheme booklets provided by the awarding bodies. Simply tick off the numbered assignments as you do them. Then, when you've completed this book, you can include the book together with any supporting documents you may create as you work through it in your NVQ portfolio. The simple matching technique will enable your NVQ assessor easily to locate your evidence and match it against the relevant criteria. Each assignment goes toward meeting performance criteria outlined in the elements shown.

Assignment at end of chapter	The Assignment Counts as Evidence Towards these Elements							
1	E111	E112	E121					
2 (Assignment 1)	E111	E211	E321					
2 (Assignment 2)	E112							
3	E111	E311						
4	E111	E112						
5	E111	E112	E211	E212	E213	E231		
6	E121	E122	E221	E222	E232			

E111   Specify processes for evaluating the contribution of training and development to an organization.

E112   Evaluate the contribution of training and development to an organization.

E121   Identify potential improvements to training and development in an organization.

E122   Plan the introduction of improvements to training and development in an organization.

E211   Select methods for evaluating training and development outcomes.

E212   Collect information to improve training and development programmes.

E213   Analyse information to improve training and development programmes.

E221   Identify potential improvements to training and development programmes.

E222   Plan the introduction of improvements to training and development programmes.

E231   Collect and analyse information on training and development sessions.

E232   Improve training and development sessions.

E311   Evaluate own practice.

E321   Manage relationship with colleagues.

So Why Do You Need to Know About Evaluation?

There is one basic assumption which underlies this book, the rest of the series and indeed the whole of your working life as a trainer: that training is worthwhile. Or, to put it another way, that the money, time and resources put into training represent a sound investment; that your organization is getting value for the money it spends on training.

It would be very easy for the trainer if this assumption went unquestioned — and all too often it does. I've seen a lot of trainers and training purchasers demonstrate the attitude that if the training has happened, it must have been all right, rather than ask 'Has this training met the needs of the organization and the individuals within it?' and 'Could the time and resources which have been committed to this training have been used in a better way?'.

Without the answers to these questions, you, your customers and everyone else involved is in the dark about whether your training was effective or not. That, in a nutshell, is why you need to know about evaluation; only proper evaluation can provide the answers you need so that you can prove that both the people involved and the organization itself are getting a return on their investment.

In one way it's a pity that this is the seventh book in the series, as it might seem from its position that evaluation is something you do when you've finished everything else. While there **is** a role for evaluation at the end of a particular training provision, that is only part of the whole picture; evaluation is far broader in scope and application than that. It has a part to play at every stage in the training process, starting with the original idea for a piece of training and going right through to the design and delivery phase. Besides, evaluation also has a part to play in the way you run your entire training function. You don't just provide training: you analyse needs, you develop strategies to ensure the training function is effective and efficient. Since you claim, as you must, that everything you do adds value to the organization, you must be able to back up that claim.

It is an important part of the training function's role to be able to justify its existence and its activities. Effective evaluation puts you in a position to do just that. Although you'll find that people use the term 'evaluation' in different ways, we're going back to the dictionary definition, that is:

- getting to know the **value** of something.

Evaluation is a process of using the outcome of assessment, testing and measuring in its widest sense to make one or more informed value judgements. As a trainer, you'll find yourself surrounded by people who purport to make value judgements about your performance and that of your function. You need to know about evaluation so that you can produce your own value judgements, based on the results of carefully designed and appropriate measurements, so that you can present the full and supportable picture to anyone who has an interest.

Finally, before you begin your exploration of the main sections of this book, I must stress that there is nothing alarming about evaluations. Many trainers fight shy of evaluation because they feel that weaknesses and failures may be revealed. I believe that this is a reason **for** evaluation rather than against. It's true that every evaluation I've been involved in has always shown up some point where there is room for improvement, or an area where something has been missed out. I welcome this information. Indeed, I rely on it to guide me in the future. Without it, I would be condemned to making the same mistakes over and over again. This is not the path to success. Given accurate, valid and reliable feedback, you can be sure you're well on the way to achieving continuous improvement.

Chapter 1

Reasons for Evaluation

Why do you evaluate your training? When we've asked that question on our travels in Europe and America, we've received a host of different answers. For some trainers, it is enough that they're asked to, or required to evaluate. For others, one or two key reasons stand out.

In this chapter we've pulled together a broad range of reasons for designing and implementing a sound evaluation process, and they're all valid. We can't say that they will all have equal priority in your situation, but we can state with confidence that you should not neglect any of them.

By the time you've completed this chapter, you will be able to:

- state six valid reasons why evaluation is crucial

- state, for each reason, the consequences of evaluating or not evaluating

- make a direct link between evaluation and your organization's survival and prosperity.

These are bold claims, so we'll make a start straight away.

Six Valid Reasons

Begin by exploring your own views. Write down in this box the main reasons why you evaluate training.

These are the reasons we've found to be most valid in our experience. Match yours to ours. The main reasons you evaluate are to ensure you make informed value judgements about:

- resources
- how to do better in the future and increase the effectiveness of your training programme
- the extent to which your training has helped to solve your organization's problems
- hunches you may have.

Also, evaluation enables you to:

- gain feedback
- justify the existence of the training function.

Admittedly, there's a fair degree of overlap between some of those reasons. But we're going to deal with them separately in turn now and, as we do so, you should try to judge how much your reasons for evaluating tally with ours.

The Effective Use of Resources

The good old-fashioned word 'stewardship' sums up what we mean. It's your duty to your organization to ensure you use the things which are entrusted to you responsibly, even if your organization never actually calls you to account.

Where you're not called to account, the more the pressure is really on, and you find yourself needing to prove to yourself that you have been acting in the best interests of the organization. For some people, evaluation is the only route to real peace of mind!

If you are regularly called to account, then you will need to be able to confirm the good use you have made of last year's budget if you want to maintain the same level of funding for the coming year. We know of organizations which have withdrawn part or all of the funding from training departments where the evaluations haven't proved satisfactorily that resources have been used effectively. But, don't be downcast; we also know of organizations which have increased funding to their trainers when they realized just what potential there was for effective return on their investment.

Doing Better in the Future

What questions do you need to ask if you're going to improve your training provision? Write your thoughts in here.

Evaluation has a major role to play in the training function's planning process. It should help you at least to answer these three key questions:

- What have we done?
- How well did we do it?
- How can we do better next time?

Case Study

In 1992 a major financial institution launched a training initiative to reduce the number of tiers of management. This meant the senior people were going to have to have increased levels of direct customer contact, which, for some of them, was quite a daunting prospect; they'd been purely internal administrators for years. The training function organized and implemented a major training initiative involving:

- group-based training sessions with role-plays
- video recording the staff in action with actors.

The 1992 evaluation showed that the training was successful in terms of:

- boosting morale
- customer satisfaction
- personal performance targets reached (with corresponding performance-related pay benefits).

It is also revealed that there was room for further development, in that several trainees felt either that there was too much time between training and practice — in which case they became rather nervous before customer interviews — or that real customer interviews threw up attitudes and behaviour which the training had not prepared them for. Late in 1992 the training department began selecting and skilling-up coaches to support these senior people in their customer interviews, and by the 1993 evaluation even greater improvements had been achieved.

The key point to note is that 'doing better' does not imply a low base. The basic premise I work to is that there is always room for improvement. Effective evaluation will help you decide where the improvement can occur and the resources required to achieve it, and whether the benefits actually do justify the resources. While there is room for improvement, there is room for evaluation to show you the way.

Solving Your Organization's Problems

There is a direct logical link which joins your evaluation of training to your organization's problems — but we're not saying that you can solve all of them. At the beginning of book 4 in this series — *Identifying Training Needs* — you saw how a training needs analysis is in fact part of a wider problem-solving exercise; that it is possible to look at an organization's problems, identify those which have a training solution and those which do not, and then proceed to take the training measures necessary to address the identified training need. It is only evaluation which can show to what extent you have solved the training aspect of the problem, and enable you to find out new ways of achieving a more complete solution in the future.

Confirming Hunches

How often have you been asked about some aspect of your training provision and replied, 'I think it would work better if . . . '?

It's quite natural that in the course of your career you will develop 'instincts' about things. Of course, they're not really instincts at all. It's your mind unconsciously processing all the information it received in the light of the sum of its experiences. The success or otherwise of these hunches will depend on a number of things:

- your level of creativity
- your level of experience
- the amount of successful hunches you've had in the past.

The point is that you won't actually know whether your hunch was a success — and if so, how great a success — unless you evaluate.

Obtaining Feedback

Feedback is always important. We've heard it argued that once a piece of training has been evaluated and proved successful, there's no need to evaluate it any more, but we disagree strongly, and we have case study evidence to back up our point.

But before we move on to that — why do *you* think continuous feedback is important in the case of established courses? Write you answer in here.

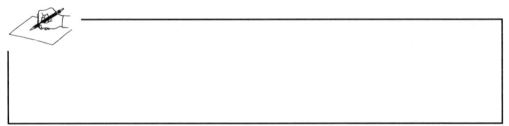

Continuous feedback is vital for this reason: while your training provision may remain constant, the needs of your trainees may not.

Case Study

Lew Olsen's induction courses were very thorough, and initial evaluations revealed that they were really hitting the mark. He stopped the evaluations, and for three years everything was fine, but in year four he started getting the sort of feedback none of us like to receive:

the course was 'boring', it went over 'old ground' and managers reported that the trainees were starting work in the organization with a real attitude problem. Line managers asked what Lew was doing differently this year, and of course, he replied there had been no changes, and attributed the complaints to a particularly bad and poorly motivated intake. Next year the problem got worse, and Lew decided to evaluate.

He discovered that the local colleges had started to run 'practical office skills' courses and that the youngsters starting in the organization had all been signing up for these courses in a bid to get off to a good start when they began work. Many of the people on his tried and tested induction course had already learned the key points before they arrived, and considered the induction course boring and repetitious.

There are many examples of courses which have failed to adapt to the changing needs of the trainees — and, consequently, those of the people who purchase the training — and we recommend regular, ongoing evaluation to avoid this situation.

We also need to state clearly that new ideas must always be evaluated, as must the 'hunches' we referred to on page 19.

Justifying the Existence of the Training Function

You may feel that we've already addressed this issue under all the other reasons, but we've separated it out to make one important point.

So far you've been justifying the training, not the training function. Evaluation can be used to show how the in-house training function is a most effective use of resource as opposed to, say, calling in outside specialist training providers. These external providers could, presumably, offer a very similar service to the one which you provide, so:

- where's the difference?
- in what ways is your service better?
- in what ways is your service more cost-effective?
- are there ways in which you can specialize in the areas you deliver most appropriately and farm out work to specialists in other areas? And would this make for a really effective use of funds?

It has been our experience that most large training functions follow a path of co-operation with external consultants. There could be, to pick an extreme example, a situation where an external consultant has access to high-specification video recording equipment which could be of use in marketing or sales training. Only evaluation would tell you whether you would get better value for money if you used you own hand-held video equipment or paid the consultants to bring in their gear and, of course, their expertise in using it. Remember, cost is not the only factor in a value for money equation.

Your host organization is unlikely to be sentimental in its regard for the training function. If it assumes that it can get better value for money by closing you down — or even that the risks of closing you down are worth taking — then it will probably do so. Evaluation is a very powerful weapon in your armoury when it comes to ensuring your future contribution to the organization.

Priorities

Now that you've looked at all six of our reasons for evaluating, you can see how great the correlation is between our thoughts and yours as expressed on page 15. Then you can move on to work out what your priority areas are. Some trainers find themselves in, or inherit, quite precarious situations, in which case evaluations tend to be 'defensive': the stress is on justifying the function's existence and looking for ways of improving next year. This could lead to an increased amount of time being spent evaluating what the training function does, and correspondingly less on the training itself.

Others are more sure of their position. They have the confidence to innovate and experiment. You can't get to a position like this unless your ongoing evaluations are thorough and provide satisfactory feedback — so for trainers in the position, gaining feedback and confirming hunches are going to be the key areas of evaluation.

But all trainers will have to address all six areas as they evaluate; the priority is up to you.

Use the space below to work out your priorities when it comes to evaluation.

Area	Reason why this is a priority evaluation area

Summary

In this first chapter you saw that understanding the reasons why evaluating is necessary can motivate you to evaluate effectively. You looked in turn at six reasons for evaluation.

First, evaluation makes for good use of resources. The pressure to use resources well can come from your own moral nature, in organizations where you are left to your own devices, or from the need to account for the money you spend, which is the case most of the time. In truth, most trainers are keen on making good use of their resources for moral and for practical reasons.

Second, evaluation can enable you to do better in the future. This is not to say that you've been failing in the past; but good trainers realize there is always room for improvement.

Third, it can help to solve your organization's problems. Given that the primary purpose of the training function is to address those organizational problems which have a training solution, then the logical link is clear. Evaluation can show to what extent training is solving the problems and can point the way towards more appropriate solutions if necessary.

Fourth, it can confirm hunches you may have. Experienced trainers often have good ideas for improvements, and evaluating these will enable you to build on this ability and use it to the maximum.

Fifth, evaluation is the only really satisfactory means of getting feedback. Remember, it's not just new ideas which need evaluating.

Last, you saw how evaluation can justify the existence of the training function. In a world where the training you provide could conceivably be provided by other, external suppliers, you will find it essential to highlight just what makes your service better value.

Different trainers will put different priorities on each of the above points but you should be very wary of neglecting any of them.

Assignment:

Look at the evaluations which your training department has completed over the last 12 months.

List, on a separate piece of paper, which of the six areas in Chapter 1 were addressed in those evaluations, and also note down their priority order, if any is apparent.

If you find there are any areas not covered, (a) note them down and (b) write down how your current position may have been weakened by this omission. If you find that the priority of previous evaluations doesn't match your needs, note down what you believe would be a more appropriate order.

Discuss the findings of this research with your colleagues and get their views.

Features of an Evaluation

Now that you've seen the reasons why it's essential to evaluate, we believe you'll be keen to find out exactly what an evaluation is.

We recommend a very methodical approach to this issue, because the layman would tend to define evaluations in terms of what they do rather than what they are. For you to do likewise could lead you astray; you could become embroiled in the doing of an evaluation without a thorough knowledge of the principles of what the evaluation actually is, and, honestly, that can cause problems for you.

By the time you have finished this chapter, you will be able to:

- list the key features of an evaluation
- explain the terms used to describe the key features of an evaluation
- analyse your own evaluations in the light of what you have learnt about the key features.

Validity

The first and most crucial feature of an evaluation is validity, which means it must **do** what it **says it will do**. If an evaluation has on its stated aim that it will measure the value to the organization of a specific training team, then, it must do so, or the consequences can be serious.

The following case study illustrates what can happen if even part of your evaluation is **invalid**.

Case Study

The training department in a goods depot trained staff to take stock every Friday afternoon. The processes were explained and rehearsed, potential problems were explored and coped with, everything was fine, and at the end of the course there was an evaluation which covered all the aspects of the course: the time people spent training, costs in terms of down-time, and analysis of savings made as a result of increased accuracy and punctuality, trainer time and resources, and an assessment of what the people had actually learned.

It was a thorough evaluation, but . . . one Friday afternoon when there was, unusually, a panic on, the three people due to take stock simply didn't. They had 'more important' things to do and just left the task undone. Next week there was unbridled chaos as the computer systems tried to cope with out-of-date information being inputted on the wrong date, and orders went astray, customers were unhappy, and there was a good deal of egg on some very important faces.

Even though this is the middle of a case study, you might like to try and guess what exactly went wrong. Write your answer in here.

No one had explained to the stocktakers why it was important to take stock on a Friday afternoon. They had simply assumed that stocktaking was something you did when you weren't that busy, and that if you were busy on Friday, you could forget it.

The evaluation was invalid. The organization thought it was getting for its money a team of stocktakers who knew what to do and knew why they were doing it — but this second part of the package wasn't there. Thus the evaluation which was supposed to be so thorough that the trainers and the organization could base all their future judgements on it wasn't that thorough at all: a question which should have been asked, namely: 'Do these people know why they are performing this task?' simply wasn't asked at all.

In this particular case, the evaluation was invalidated by real life rearing its head several months into the training programme, and you can imagine that the consequences for the trainers were dire; all their other evaluations were undermined, because the organization had lost confidence in them.

The flaw in this particular evaluation was that it did not spot the missing training objective. There are other possible flaws in evaluations, and here we provide a list of the more common ones so that you can beware the pitfalls which have embarrassed trainers in the past.

1   The data are processed wrongly

Imagine a situation where trainees need to get 90 per cent on a test to demonstrate competence, and one trainee manages precisely that. The 10 per cent he didn't get, however, contained the most crucial and vital elements of learning without which he could not possibly be competent. The data processing should have given proper weighting to the most important elements.

2   The data are missing

It frequently happens that in analysing costs various items are overlooked, for example:

- trainee time
- trainer time (preparation, delivery and follow-up)
- comparative costs of alternative solutions.

3. Assumptions which underlie the whole training programme are unidentified

It's a good discipline to make explicit all the assumptions you're working from when you prepare your evaluation. Otherwise they may perpetuate themselves until it's too late. For example, if you're working with trainees who have no experience — say so. If you're not sure of the level of experience: find out!

Objectivity

When you evaluate, you must remain as objective as possible. Evaluation can be seen as a two-stage operation: designing the research instruments and analysing the data.

Of these two stages, it is easier to be objective in the first; for example, if you're preparing a list of questions to test whether the knowledge, skills and attitudes you think have been learned actually have been learned, then it is easy to maintain a distance, because you're not at that stage concerned about what the answers will be. That's fine; it's as it should be.

What is it which makes it harder to be objective when you're analysing the data? Write your answer in this box.

When you're analysing data, you have an idea of what you expect the data to be telling you. This basic assumption that you may have — that the training has been enjoyed; that it has hit the mark; or whatever — may cloud your interpretation of the facts. Thus if your training is given, say, seven out of ten for stimulation by those who attend the course, you could interpret it positively or negatively — it's up to you. We recommend that you apply the following criteria to your interpretation of all the facts:

- would a stern critic of the training agree with your interpretation?

- have you given all the points the weighting they deserve?

- will your interpretation of the facts stand the test of time?

Involvement

Evaluation is like the rest of training: it is something you do **with** people, not **to** them.

This fact has two major implications for the way you do your evaluations. First, it's not going to be a solo act on your part. You don't just observe people, obtain statistics and then disappear for a week or two to concoct a report. Nor do you ask your trainees to tell their managers what they think of the course and leave it at that. Evaluation needs everyone's support.

Second, it will require some skill on your part to get the level of commitment you need from everyone. You can't just ask them to help you evaluate — the chances are they won't know what you're talking about, and even if they do, they may well think that it's your job and that you're just trying to pass a boring job on to them.

A Plan of Campaign

Any successful evaluation will involve three perspectives: yours, your trainees' and their managers' (who may well be your customers). Once you've identified and named the individuals who are to be involved in your evaluation process, there are three stages to be gone through in getting them 'on board':

- encourage understanding
- sell the benefits of support
- charm.

Encouraging understanding means that you will have to inform everyone concerned what evaluation is and what their particular role in it is to be. Stress all the time that it is a partnership and you won't go far wrong.

Selling the benefits of support is fairly self-explanatory. As with nearly everything else in life, if people understand what's in it for them, they will go along with it. If they don't they won't. The benefits of evaluation to the trainee are:

- confirmation that their training has in fact equipped them for the job
- genuine insights into the nature of training which will stand them in good stead for their future learning experiences
- reassurance that their needs are being met by a professional training function both willing and able to respond to any problems or omissions the evaluation may throw up
- credit in the eyes of their manager for being so co-operative.

The benefits to the manager are:

- a meaningful, accurate evaluation
- reassurance that their needs are being taken seriously
- the opportunity to influence the future training provision as it affects them
- credit in the eyes of their trainees, because they are being seen to take the training seriously.

Charm is you secret weapon. Despite all the benefits being spelt out, there may be one or two individuals whom you need to co-operate, but who aren't yet willing. Make them feel special; explain to them that they're the lynch-pin of the whole operation; tell them you're grateful, and that their name will be noted when your evaluation report goes 'right to the very top . . . '. They may say that flattery gets you nowhere, but it's worth a try!

Feasibility

Write in this box two ways in which your evaluation must be feasible.

The answers we came up with were that your evaluation must be:

- cost-effective

    and

- practical.

The data you collect must be important enough to justify the expense of gathering them. It is possible to become a sort of 'evaluation junkie' and gather more and more data, when there is, realistically, always a cut-off point. You'll know when you've got to that point because you'll find that all your new data are merely confirming what you can already prove, so you might as well stop.

The methods you adopt must be practical — and, as a working definition of 'practical' we suggest this: that the methods you use must be within the ability and experience of the people who are using them, and within the capacity of the organization to deal with. So, for example, there is no point in opting for a high-tech cross-referencing technique if there is no one available with the requisite computer skills, and anyway, the hardware and/or software isn't up to the job. This may sound an obvious point, but there are occasions when the ideal way of evaluating just isn't feasible — but people try it anyway, on the basis that achieving a proportion of the ideal solution is better than achieving all of a not-so-good solution. In our experience, a thorough evaluation using modest methods always outweighs a patchy evaluation using sophisticated methods.

Reliability

In many standard texts, reliability is mentioned alongside validity as one of the two key features of an evaluation; in this text we're mentioning it last of five — but that is not to dispute its importance.

First, people are going to rely on your evaluations when it comes to making future decisions. So your evaluation has to be reliable, or it's completely useless — in fact, worse than useless, because people will try to rely on it, fail, and suffer positive harm as a consequence. But what is it that makes an evaluation reliable? We like to look at it like this. If your evaluation is reliable, you should be able to:

- confirm its findings by another means
- give the data to another trainer who would reach similar conclusions.

Sometimes it happens that trainers who have been subjective when they analysed their data produce results which are not reliable; if you're at all worried that this might be true in your case, get someone to check it over for you — preferably someone who is not emotionally involved in the outcome of the evaluation.

If there are no people to ask to help in this way, you should build into your evaluation what we could call a binocular approach: don't rely on one method of data-gathering and data-processing: use two. Each method should confirm the other.

To exercise your imagination for a while, detail in the box below what you would do if your reliability check revealed differences. Say, for example, you looked at the data and reached one conclusion, and a colleague reached a different conclusion. Write your thoughts in here.

There is a logical way to approach all discrepancies of this type. Here is the sequence of actions:

1. Focus in on the discrepancies

2. Identify the reasons for the discrepancies

3. If you can't find the reason, go back to basic principles: what information were you trying to obtain from the data? If you can't find that information reliably by asking the question you asked or using the method you used, then find another means of getting what you need.

If you follow this sequence you will be able to identify inconsistencies of interpretation by stage 2, and errors in evaluative technique (should you need to go that far) in stage 3.

Summary

In Chapter 2 you have seen that a successful evaluation must have certain features if it is to do its job. It must have:

- **validity** — which means being based on sufficient relevant and accurate evidence to enable you to make a sound judgement

- **objectivity** — you must be careful not to let your desired interpretation of the data interfere with your judgement

- **involvement** — evaluations are never a solo operation; just as the training is a shared experience so should the evaluation be. This also helps to reinforce the view that evaluation is part of training

- **feasibility** — sometimes the ideal method of gathering and analysing data is a non-starter for purely practical reasons: you may not have the skills, the resources or the money. Besides this, you should be careful not to go into unnecessary detail

- **reliability** — since people are going to rely on your evaluation, you should be sure its conclusions are sound. This means that you should be able to confirm its findings by other means, or give the data to a colleague who would reach similar conclusions.

Assignment 1:

Draw up a list of the people whom you would ideally like to involve in the evaluation of your training, and note for each name the role you would like them to play and why. Remember to include someone, if possible, who can help you at the reliability checking stage of the operation.

You will need to re-visit and refine this list as you go through the remaining chapters of this book. New ideas for specific people's contributions will surface as you read.

Ultimately you should take a tape-recorder to a meeting between yourself and the people on your list and record the proceedings as you explain to them what it is you need, and encourage them to help.

Assignment 2:

Take a recent evaluative exercise and identify in it the five features we have described in this chapter. If you feel that any of the features are missing or under-emphasized, say which they are and write down what you will do to correct the situation before your next evaluation.

Chapter 3

Evaluating the Training Function

There are more opportunities for you to evaluate than merely at that point where you deem a certain item of training to be complete. There are the stages of design, development and delivery of each item of training which you will look at in detail in Chapter 4. And there is the way the training function operates — the other things you do in the background, at a strategic level, to enable your training to be designed and delivered — all this needs to be evaluated. This chapter outlines what in these areas ought — and ought not — to be evaluated.

By the time you have worked through this chapter, you will be able to:

- list those areas of your training function which need to be evaluated

- state the benefits of evaluation in each case

- state the dangers of failing to evaluate

- describe the point at which evaluation becomes nothing more than a self-perpetuating exercise and should cease

- identify occasions where you evaluate automatically without being aware of it.

It has been our experience of the points in this chapter that they are often neglected by hard-pressed trainers who concentrate on the delivery of training. We are also aware that the time devoted to evaluating the function itself can be time well-spent; you could well find opportunities to save time and effort, and to become a more cost-effective operation. In a world where many trainers judge their success by the amount of hours they put in to meet deadlines, a spot of evaluation of the function could help take the pressure off and enable you to concentrate your energies on providing what the customer needs.

Value for Money

Trainers who only evaluate the training they design and provide are not always presenting a true picture of their cost-base to their host organization. For many people this is not at first sight a problem: for example, where all departments have a certain proportion of the budgets earmarked for 'administrative costs', and provided that you don't exceed those costs, you're all right. No questions are asked, and it is assumed that you're basically working efficiently.

This leads us to two points. First, if your administrative costs aren't looked at, is that any reason not to try to ensure that you are none the less making the best use of your resources? Businesses face cut-throat competition from rivals so that any wastefulness will ultimately be punished, and even non-profit-making organizations owe it to their sponsors and the people they serve to exercise good stewardship. Yes, there's that old-fashioned word again, but it's really relevant.

Second, not all departments get away with not having their costs analysed. Some are scrutinized annually, others every two years or in some form of rotation. Taken all in all, it is essential to take a value-for-money look at everything you do.

Which areas of your activity do you think could benefit from some measure of evaluation? Write your suggestions in here.

We believe that these areas are particularly high on costs, time and effort, and could well be worth evaluating:

- your strategic planning
- your needs analyses
- the way you categorize your learners
- the way you select your training methods and, of course
- the way you implement your training.

The last point deserves — and gets — a chapter all to itself. You should look at the others in turn now.

Strategic Planning

Case Study

Leo Suppewicz was training manager in a large communications organization. He was appointed shortly after the organization decided to restructure its business: fixed hierarchies were out, teams were in. Leo saw straight away the need for interpersonal skills training which this major change caused, and costed out the options. The ideal solution was too expensive and, in fact, so low was the standing of the training department that he only grudgingly got 10 per cent of what he asked for. Working within these financial constraints, he instigated a cascade system of training throughout the organization, where selected individuals got what he called the 'Rolls-Royce' training, and had then to pass it on.

By the time the training filtered through to the furthest extremes of the organization — which was nearly two years later — most of the valuable information was lost, and the new ideas and attitudes were making few inroads into the existing culture.

The post-training evaluation showed that the training had not delivered what it promised, and Leo's standing in the organization took a downward turn.

In terms of value for money, Leo's training was a success: the organization hadn't paid much, and they hadn't got much. The two sides of the equation balanced exactly. What Leo should have done (and it's easy to be wise after the event) was to plan strategically. A strategic plan is supposed to enable you to provide your organization with the training it needs in the way it needs it. The very fact that it is strategic implies that there may not be any immediate benefit, but that in the long term it will pay dividends.

Leo's plan should have looked like this:

Question	Answer
What is the aim of the training function?	To provide the training the organization needs in the way it needs it.
So what training does it need?	Interpersonal skills training through video, booklets, face-to-face and follow-up coaching.
How can I enable this to happen?	Obtain sufficient funds, and plan courses.
What obstacles are there?	Low status of training department; not trusted with money.
How to remedy this?	Raise profile of training department through publicity and successful completion of less ambitious projects.
What are my next steps?	To plan awareness-raising events, produce a news-sheet and plan improvements to existing training provision (eg, induction).

Given a properly prepared strategic plan (of which this is a mere overview), what would have been the questions for Leo to ask in order to *evaluate* it? Write your answers in here.

The questions should be:

- what was the plan meant to achieve?
- did it achieve it?
- if there are differences between intended achievement and actual achievement, how can these be remedied?
- could the strategy have been worked more cost-effectively?

It's possible that you can already see what we meant earlier when we referred to 'automatic evaluation'. The plan was meant to enable the trainer to implement interpersonal skills training for the people, and if the board had, 12 months later, provided the funds needed then it is clear that the plan would have had a better chance of success.

The evaluation is, of course, not always so simple. As a trainer you could find yourself looking in detail at whether, say, the news-sheet element of your profile-raising plan was more cost-effective than your upgrading of your current induction-training provision. If you are being called to account for every penny you spend, you will need to do this sort of thing, but often, where your criterion is simply success or failure, you may not need to.

Needs Analyses

The book *Identifying Training Needs* in this series demonstrates a tried and tested method of carrying out a training needs analysis (TNA).

At the end of the TNA you should evaluate what you've done so far. Similar questions to those asked at the end of the strategic planning will help you focus your mind, but basically, you need to know whether your TNA was an accurate one or not.

There are many points at which a TNA can go off the rails, and there are correspondingly many points at which evaluation is appropriate. Don't panic — the evaluation technique is very simple and effective: at the end of every stage of the TNA you check back with the person who commissions the TNA that you are exactly on the right lines. This grid outlines exactly what we mean:

Needs analysis stage	Evaluation question to be asked before progressing to next stage
1. Identify the client	Person 'x' is going to pay for this TNA and has the authority to implement its findings: is that correct?
2. Clarify the expectations	This written document contains all the details of what the client expects and the parameters within which I may work. Will the client sign it as accurate?
3. Design the programme	Does the client approve this plan?
4. Arrange access to data	Do I have permission to get information on these subjects from these people?
5. Collect the data	I have collected the data; does the client approve? Has the client any further requirements?
6. Make sense of the findings	This is the interpretation I am putting on the data: is this appropriate in terms of usefulness and the client's expectations?

7. Produce a draft report	This is what I propose to say and how I propose to say it: does the client approve?
8. Produce and distribute a final report and recommendations	These are the people who need to know the results of the TNA. Is the list complete?

It is possible to look on each of these questions as merely 'protecting your own back'; but in fact you are giving the client — the ultimate arbiter of value for money — an opportunity to check at every stage that you are being cost-effective and to ask questions.

Categorizing Learners

Understanding How People Learn — book 3 in this series — explored this area in some depth, and it became clear that there are different kinds of learner, for example, theorists and activists, and that each type of learner responds more readily to a specific style of training.

Part of your task as a trainer is to analyse the way your people learn and then:

- either take action to develop your people so that their repertory of learning skills is increased
- or adapt your training style so that it is more appropriate to your learners' existing repertory.

These actions need to be evaluated so that you know for certain whether you've taken the best action you possibly can. On one hand it is clear that all individuals have a capacity to learn in many different ways, using many different learning strategies, and the more ways each individual can feel comfortable with, the better at learning the individual will become. This would point you in the direction of personal development for all individuals. On the other hand, in certain circumstances — say, in a research laboratory where there will be a preponderance of learners well versed in theoretical and experimental styles, it would seem to be a more effective use of the money at your disposal to adapt the courses to fit the learners. So which action do you take?

The best answer is to try both — and evaluate. Simply put some learners through some learning development and then ask the questions relating to what you were trying to achieve and whether it worked cost-effectively or not (which will involve you in measuring costs in terms of money, time and effort, as well as benefits in terms of motivation and ability to do the job) and then repeat the exercise for a situation where you decide to amend the course.

Selecting Training Methods

When you're evaluating this part of your training function, you must be careful to separate out the issues of whether the training method has worked and how you selected the training method, although the two do hang together very closely.

Value for money, when it comes to selecting training methods, is a matter of two sides of a mathematical formula. On one side of the formula there is the time, effort and cash devoted to selecting the training method, and on the other . . .

What do you believe should be on the other side of the formula? Write your answers in here. We believe there are several items you could include.

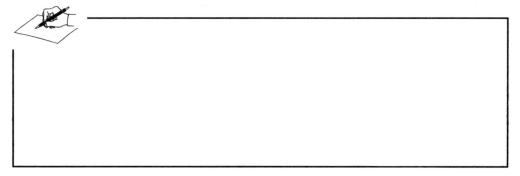

There are three main elements to put on the other side:

- effectiveness
- durability
- contribution to the organization.

Effectiveness is of course a key consideration. A long time spent selecting a training method may well be justified if the method does what it is supposed to. If it doesn't, then the effort put into selecting it was wasted.

Durability is also a key, because if you light upon a training method which can be used again and again with only minor modifications, then the selection process need not be repeated and will pay for itself many times over.

It is possible that a training method delivers the goods in terms of reaching its training objectives, but that the complete package only makes a minimal **contribution to the future survival and prosperity of the organization**. In this situation you will at least have the consolation of knowing that your selection technique was accurate, but unfortunately, the time spent selecting it was wasted because the whole exercise was misguided.

Look now at the complete formula.

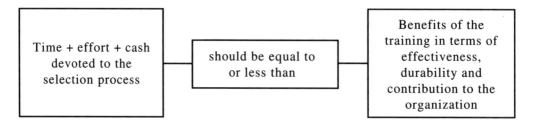

Evaluation for its Own Sake?

Apart from the implementation of training, the other main task of the training function is evaluation. And, as with other tasks, evaluation can be done well or badly: but should you evaluate your own evaluation?

The answer is both yes and no. There is only one acceptable measure for the evaluation of evaluation. If you've shown how what you have done provides value for money (or otherwise), then your evaluation is a success. If you could prove the same point for less money or using less resources, then you should do so.

And that, really is an end of it. You could go on evaluating everything, but this would lead you round in ever decreasing circles. Evaluation has its part to play at various points in the training cycle, but it is neither the largest nor the most dominant part on any occasion. It is a support, a check, an opportunity to correct or balance. In a nutshell — don't overdo it. The expense of evaluating must be justified by its results.

Summary

In Chapter 3 you've seen how important it is to evaluate not only the training that you implement, but also the training function itself. Within the function, you saw these points merited particular evaluation:

- your strategic planning — because it is possible to waste a lot of time, money and resources if your overall plan is flawed

- your needs analyses — because there are many places where a TNA can go astray, and it's a straightforward task to check with your customer at every key stage

- the way you categorize your learners — because you need to know whether it is more cost-effective to develop your learners or to adapt your training methods

- the way you select your training methods — because you're not providing value for money if you select methods which don't work or if the selection process is too long or expensive for the benefits the training brings.

Our final point was that evaluation can be taken to excess — and, of course, we recommend against it! Evaluations of evaluations can go on for ever, and they can end up being a drain on your limited resources.

Assignment:

Draw up a list of those responsibilities of the training function which have and have not been evaluated in the last 12 months.

If there are two or more areas which have been missed, call a meeting of your training team and decide amongst yourselves which of these areas has the greatest potential to use money and resources wisely or wastefully, and use the results of your discussion to create a priority evaluation hit-list for your training function.

You will be able to use this list in conjunction with the evaluative techniques you will meet later to carry out the evaluations you need.

Evaluating Your Training

This chapter is the backbone of the book. In the last analysis, either the training that you provide **is** valuable to the organization and the people within it, or it **isn't** — and this chapter is first of all about the **things you need to look at** in order to measure the value (or otherwise) of training; and secondly about the **times and occasions** in the design and delivery stage at which it is appropriate to look at them.

We are not yet looking in any detail at the ways of measuring the value and the techniques you need to apply. These points come later. First and most crucially you need a thorough understanding of what features you need to consider and the correct moments to consider them.

By the time you have worked through this chapter you will be able to:

- list the aspects of your organization which should be affected by training

- specify the questions you need to ask which will enable you ultimately to measure the value of your training

- identify the stages in your training at which it is appropriate to ask those questions.

These are broad objectives, and each will contain a wealth of detail, as you'll see in the course of this chapter.

Where to Start

The best evaluation techniques in the world won't be effective if they are applied in the wrong area at the wrong time. It follows that the correct place to start evaluation is at the level of basic principles: and that means identifying the ways in which your organization could potentially profit from training.

In true open learning style, we're going to turn that question round so that you have to think about it; but before we do, think first about some of the difficulties that arise. In some aspects of your organization the impact of training will be easier to measure than in others, due mainly to reasons we explored in book 1 of this series — *Understanding the Training Function.* There are certain benefits of training which are eminently measurable and visible, and which have immediate effect. There are other benefits which are more subtle and whose effects take perhaps rather longer to manifest themselves.

In what aspects of your organization do you think that training ought to have an effect? List them in the box below and begin with the more immediate, visible and easily measured aspects — where the training input is easier to discern — and end with those aspects which are less tangible and slower to appear.

We have found that the areas where training benefits become most immediately apparent are all related to job performance.

The less tangible benefits relate to the way the whole organization:

- thinks
- feels
- acts
- reacts.

Measuring the Impact of Training on Job Performance

You might expect that all the key questions relating to the value of training should be asked at the workplace, but real life isn't as simple as that. Of course, it is when the trainees are back at the workplace after training that they begin to make their maximum contribution to the organization, so there are questions which need to be asked there. But, as you'll see, there are also questions which are better asked in a controlled environment, say in or immediately after the training event.

The way your training is designed also impacts on job performance. Well-designed training has a much more marked and positive impact than anything poorly-designed, and there are, as you'd expect, questions to be asked about this aspect of things.

1 Learners' Job Performance as Observed at the Workplace

You would expect training to have a positive effect on the way people do their jobs. So, from the organizational perspective, you can see that it is imperative to ask these questions actually at the workplace:

- are people performing better as a result of the training?
- were learners able to apply what they learnt to their normal work?
- did the training prepare adequately for (a return to) work?

None of these questions is easy, and you'll look at ways of answering them later in the book.

For the moment, you need to recognize that job performance is not the outcome of training alone. In the box below, write down three factors which may distort the picture.

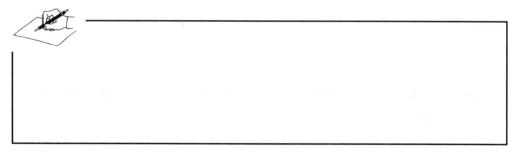

We identified a total of four major distorting factors:

- working conditions
- equipment
- motivation

  and

- supervision.

Any of these or any combination of them can conspire to impact on job performance, with the result that it can appear to make good training fail and, on occasions, poor training succeed. This clearly will distort any evaluations based wholly on questions asked at the workplace: what should, in ideal circumstances, give proof positive of the impact of training is, in fact, always going to be tainted. This problem can be tackled in a combination of ways. First, we believe that the training objectives should try to accommodate the possible variety of circumstances at the workplace. For example, you don't say that the trainee should be able to sew 13 garments an hour; rather you say that the trainee should be able to sew 13 specific garments an hour during a six-hour shift using machines x, y and z. This tightening of objectives will enable you to ask more meaningful questions at the workplace and compensate for some possible distorting factors, but it won't go the whole way. The second element in the solution to the problem is crucial, and it involves asking evaluative questions under controlled conditions.

2 Learners' Job Performance as Measured Under Controlled Conditions

'Controlled conditions' can mean anywhere under the trainer's control, for example:

- the training room
- the examination room
- the test-bench.

The question which arises first is: how can proof of learning in laboratory conditions be taken as proof of training's contribution to the organization? Write your thoughts in this box.

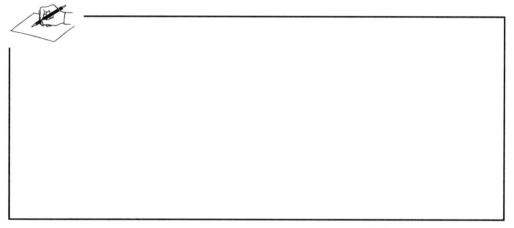

First, we have stated on many occasions through this series that an organization consists of its people and it follows that if you benefit the people by giving them the skills they need to do their job well, you are benefiting the organization. Admittedly, at an organizational level, this benefit may in part take the form of increased potential — potential which may not be realized straight away — but it's there, and it is valuable.

Second, results under controlled conditions can measure the amount of learning which has taken place. It cannot measure the success or otherwise of the application of that learning, but since things unlearnt can never be applied, proof of learning is still an important indicator of the success you've had.

This brings us to the matter of what questions to ask to ensure that learning has taken place. We believe that the following list of questions covers the important ground:

- did the training meet the objectives set for it?
- how did the learners feel about the training?
- were people prepared for training?
- was the training pitched at the right level?

All of those questions merit some more detailed study.

Objectives

In *Implementing Training* you spent some time looking at the importance of objectives, and at the key descriptors of good objectives. To recapitulate the main points here for the purpose of this book: objectives make an effective end-point for a particular item of training, and if they're designed properly, they will tell you exactly what the learner should be able to do as a result of the training. This means that every objective should state explicitly:

- what the learner should do
- the conditions under which it should be done
- the standards to be reached.

For example, 'calculate accurately one three-digit number as a percentage of another in nine examples out of ten, given five minutes, using a calculator' is a better learning objective than simply 'work out percentages'. You can see how much easier it is to evaluate.

Learners' feelings

We are never in favour of training which is entirely 'soft and friendly'. But trainees' feelings are important, because if they haven't enjoyed the course or found it relevant:

- they will not have learnt very well from it

- they will be less inclined to implement it in the workplace
- there will be an increased likelihood of their rejecting what they've learnt in favour of other, disapproved attitudes or practices.

While responses which indicate enjoyment and relevance don't guarantee successful learning, they increase the chance of it.

Trainees' preparation

If the trainees come to a training session unprepared, then they will spend the first half of the event with only a certain proportion of their mind on the subject of the course. The rest of their concentration will be expended on mentally 'catching up' with where they're supposed to be. This does not make for good learning.

The most appropriate time to ask them whether they were prepared or not is immediately on completion of the event. This is when they will be best able to tell you what would have helped them beforehand.

The level of the training

Another good indicator of whether effective learning has taken place is trainees' perception (which may be different from yours!) of the level of training they have just received. In our experience there is a strong correlation between the effectiveness of the learning and the extent to which the trainees felt that the training had been at an appropriate level. Set the level too high and you'll simply make the whole event incomprehensible. Set it too low and your audience will feel patronized and will switch off.

Of these two extremes, setting things too high is perhaps the more common fault. There are trainers around who appear to believe there is some merit in deliberately making things hard to understand so that only the brighter, highly-motivated trainees stand a chance. Unfortunately, it just doesn't work like that. We advise you to get the level right. There are stages in the development process where you can check that you're on the right track. You'll see more about this in the next chapter.

3. The Impact of Training Design

There is no point in asking the simple question: 'Was your training well-designed?' of anyone except a competent and experienced trainer, because they won't know what you mean. Yet the people with the answer to this question are (a) the customers who have commissioned the training, and (b) the trainees at the end of the training event — so they will need help in coming to grips with the size of the issues which training design raises. You'll see how to ask the questions so that people can face the issues in the next chapter.

Think about the training design yourself for a minute or two and then write down what questions you think are the crucial ones to answer in this area. Use this box for your thoughts.

We believe these are the key questions relating to training design:

- were the training needs properly identified?
- were the learning objectives relevant?
- were the performance standards correctly set?
- were the right priorities established?

We mentioned the issue of training needs identification in the previous chapter, but as you can see, when it comes to evaluating training design, the needs are only part of the picture. It is possible that you have followed your customer's instructions to the letter, and delivered every aspect of your training exactly as required by the people who pay your wages — and yet still have got it wrong. Evaluating your design enables you to get right to the very root of things, to allow you to check that you were actually training people in the correct skills, knowledge and attitudes in the correct way.

A word before we leave this point: don't worry that you will be expected to take responsibility for all training which has missed the mark. It frequently happens when training design is evaluated that people realize that the world has changed; that training which was perfectly suited to last year's situation is now a little out of date. If so, good. You're in a position to upgrade, or — which is even better — to include an element of flexibility into your training so that it will be able to cope with changing situations in the future.

Interim Summary (1)

In this exploration of the aspects of your organization which training can be expected to impact on, we lighted first of all on the area of **job performance**.

To measure the impact of training on this important area, you'll need to ask questions about:

- the improvement measured and observed at the workplace
- the effectiveness of the learning as measured under controlled conditions and
- the design of your training.

You are now ready to move on to look at the ways in which other areas of your organization are affected by training, and what questions you need to ask to measure the effect.

Less Tangible Benefits

The list of less tangible benefits you can expect training to have on your organization was as follows. Training should have a positive effect on the way your organization:

- thinks
- feels
- acts
- reacts.

These things are intangible, but we need to measure them because they are very real. In fact they are the ultimate justification for the existence of training. Unfortunately, the contribution of training to these things can be difficult to assess, for one main reason: there are so many variables which can affect an organization's performance and the attitudes of the people within that organization.

Think of five or six of those variables, and write them in the box below.

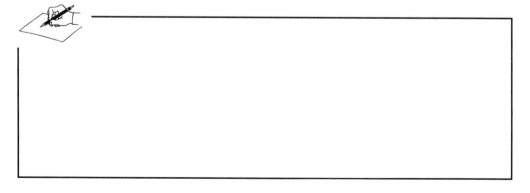

Here are the variables we came up with. See how yours compare:

- the organization's structure and hierarchy
- its products
- its technology
- the fear of technology
- fear of recession
- pay and incentive levels.

Any or all of these factors could — and do — affect the way different organizations think and feel.

It is possible to evaluate the effects of each of these individual factors, but the costs in terms of money, time and other resources are such that it is beyond the scope of the average training department. Slightly more feasible — but still expensive and only suitable for large organizations is the use of control groups to separate out training from other factors and evaluate it on its own.

Control groups are groups of people parallel to the trainee group but who receive no special training at all; their progress and performance and their attitudes and reactions are monitored alongside others who receive training. The difference can only be attributed to training, because all other factors are the same.

Not everybody is in the fortunate position of having an organization large enough for evaluations of this nature. There are none the less other things you can do in any size of organization to get an accurate indication of how far and how profoundly training is affecting these intangible elements.

1 Apply the Pyramid Principle

Even in these days of flattened hierarchies and structural review, most organizations have a small number of people at the top making important strategic decisions, and larger numbers of people at the bottom carrying out the day-to-day tasks and making sure the organization functions.

Trainers who train individuals at the top can be relatively sure that they get more influence per hour of training than they would if they were training at the bottom. The word is this: influence the people at the top and you influence everyone — albeit indirectly. The subject matter of the training is crucial here. Training in team motivation and decision-making will enable key people to have a major effect, as will other subjects which the key people can actually **use**. Training key people in routine administration, for example, — and, then expecting them to 'pass the training on' — will be less effective. Training which is passed on becomes diluted.

2 Monitor Key Events

This is not an easy approach to carry out scientifically, but it will provide you with some useful data if you can find a way of tackling it. The essence is to be aware of key incidents at work which can legitimately be attributed to the impact of training.

Write in this box two key incidents which could occur in your organization, and which, if they did occur, would be attributable to training.

Compare these examples from our experience. Admittedly, these may come from different areas of operation from those you're familiar with, but they will serve for purposes of comparison:

- the accident rate falls below a given level
- sales volumes increase dramatically.

When you spot a key event like this, you should take all reasonable steps to ensure that it has not been caused by anything other than training. This may mean making sure that there has not been a major advertising campaign or the like, which would serve only to muddy your waters.

3. Remember Poor Training Doesn't Achieve Much

We don't want to go over old ground, but we must make it clear that there is little chance of your training having any positive effect on your organization if it is failing to have an effect on the way people do their jobs. Thus training which does not pass muster when judged against the criteria you looked at in the first half of this chapter should not trouble you too greatly in terms of its intangible effects.

Such intangible effects as there are will be negative, and you should avoid them:

- poor standing of the training department
- reluctance to train
- suspicion of innovation
- low morale.

Interim Summary (2)

In this second part of the chapter you have looked at why it is important to try to evaluate the intangible effects which training has on your organization. You also saw the difficulties which may prevent you from carrying out an accurate evaluation, notably:

- the number of variables in any evaluation equation at this level
- the difficulties of setting up a control experiment.

Next you saw ways in which you can gain significant results from an evaluation at this level:

- by applying the pyramid principle
- by monitoring key events.

As a final point you saw that only training which impacts on job performance can go on to affect the organization in a positive, but tangible way.

We shall conclude this chapter with an examination of the points at which you should ask questions if you are to get meaningful results.

When to Ask Evaluative Questions

To take the simplest view, you should ask evaluative questions 'all the time', but unfortunately the simple view is, in this case, not very informative. As a competent trainer you need a more structured approach to evaluative questioning, and that is what this section of the chapter proposes to give you. In our experience it has been very helpful to divide evaluation into three broad phases.

Use the box below to write down what you believe would be a suitable division into three phases, and state briefly what you think should happen in each phase. Focus on just one element of your training provision as you compose your answer.

We suggest this division:

- a trial phase — where new methods, approaches, courses or materials are tested on a small scale before full operation

- an ongoing phase — possibly throughout the whole training process, when either the whole of training or particular aspects of it are carefully analysed with a view to modification

- a final phase — which looks back on the training process and its outcomes, and looks forward to fresh needs and new training initiatives.

There is a good deal of information for you to absorb about each of these phases — so much, in fact, that as well as going through them one by one now, you'll see that we subdivide the first two phases into two halves to make the whole thing more accessible.

When to Ask Questions (1) — The Trial Phase

This is the early, tentative phase of development. As we mentioned above, the evaluation process at this stage divides into two. The fist part is a **developmental test**. This is usually a small-scale and quite informal trial of a sample set of materials, exercises or activities. You can carry out a developmental test like this in artificial conditions, and this will in many cases enable you to get important feedback in a form you can access at an early date. You will be able to tell whether:

- your material is fine — in which case, you should carry on

- your material could be all right if you made certain changes

- you need to go back to the drawing board.

Because this test happens at such an early stage, you can use the results of it to change tack if necessary without incurring too much cost. From this it becomes clear that the timing of the developmental test is crucial. Do it too early, and the materials will not be properly enough formed for anyone to draw any meaningful conclusions from evaluating them. Do it too late and the conclusions will be valid and reliable, but reacting to those conclusions may be an expensive job.

It is also important to note that the sample set you choose to test must be selected with some care. While a straightforward sample of non-contentious material may have the advantage that it can be prepared quickly, it has the greater disadvantage that you cannot infer success or appropriateness from it.

Case Study

A major multinational chemical producer approached its training team to ask for materials to train people so that they approached the issues of safety, health and the environment in the same way: namely with the same degree of commitment and conviction and following the same procedures as far as their different working environments allowed.

When it came to developing the materials, a senior chemist suggested that the trainers should develop something to deal with the labelling of hazardous chemicals: not because this area was more crucial than any other, but because the chemist himself had seen other people's attempts at tackling the same subject, he'd tried to tackle them himself, and every time the end result had never been satisfactory for his department's particular needs. 'If you can crack that one,' said the man, 'you can crack anything'.

The training department did crack it — so much so that the chemist called the finished article a work of genius! But we add this last point only for the sake of completeness.

We recommend that the timing of a developmental test is decided using this process:

1. Build a date for the developmental test into the design process

2. Build time to react to the developmental test into the design process, remembering that you may be involved in a significant amount of redrafting and re-working

3. Ensure that a proportion of the finished product is developed to such a degree that it can be used by a sample of your end-users and that it bears a close resemblance to the finished product.

We'll be explaining some of the methods you can use — including ways of selecting appropriate people to act as guinea-pigs — in the next chapter. For now, you should pursue the train of thought which is taking you through the timing of the various stages of evaluation; for once the developmental test is complete, you should instigate a pilot test — the second stage in the evaluation of the trial phase.

Pilot testing should be a more refined operation. If the developmental test was aimed at providing rough-and-ready results to enable you to decide whether you should progress or not, the pilot will tell you whether the training being evaluated is suitable for the target population, under normal working conditions.

Therefore, when arranging a pilot test, you should focus on:

- testing one training experience or a set of materials in whole or in part
- working with a small set of learners whose profile, taken as a group, reflects the profile of the whole target audience
- ensuring that the test takes place in conditions as near as possible to the real ones.

The secret of success of the pilot test is that its scale is small, but representative, Representativeness ensures accuracy, and smallness means that the amount of data you have to process will not get out of hand, and so you can come up with conclusions quickly.

What sort of thing would you look out for in the results of a pilot test? And what sort of action would you expect to have to take as a result of it? Answer those questions in this box.

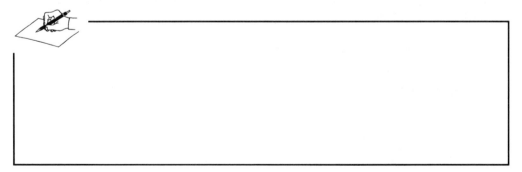

A pilot test seeks to sift out:

- weaknesses
- incongruities
- inconsistencies
- missing links.

It follows that these are the things you should be looking for.

As for the action you would expect to take, it should first of all be corrective and manageable. It is an opportunity to put things right before the whole package becomes fully operational. It is not (or it **should** not be) an opportunity to cancel the package, to delay it indefinitely, to redraft it all, or even to postpone it. If your pilot test throws up feedback which would indicate you have to take drastic actions like this, then something went seriously wrong at the developmental test stage.

It will help you to balance your developmental test and your pilot test if you see the latter as a refinement and a confirmation of the former.

When to Ask Questions (2) — the Ongoing Phase

Developmental tests and pilots should ensure that all your training meets the criteria set for it, and this is why many trainers rely on it too much. 'If it was right at the beginning, it's right for all time' seems to be the attitude. If you feel yourself tempted to think likewise, we need to remind you of that unalterable law of the world which says that if something can go wrong, it will go wrong. This leads us to two conclusions. **First**, it is vital to test out **new** training:

- in its complete and finished from
- with real learners
- in the real world.

Second — well, over to you: what do you think our second conclusion is? Write it in here.

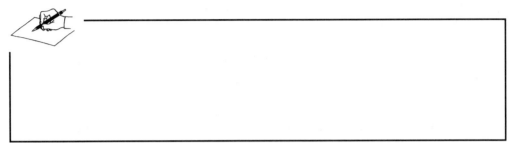

Our second conclusion is that when the training is no longer new — when it is an established part of your training provision — it should be constantly evaluated to make sure it is still doing the job it is supposed to.

You will note that by reaching these two conclusions, we have divided the ongoing evaluation effectively into two sections, which we will call **validation** and **formative evaluation**.

Validation is used to measure the effectiveness of a whole training scheme:

- in real conditions
- with a sample which is both large and representative of the whole target population.

Its purposes are wide-ranging. Without implying any priority order to them — because priorities vary from place to place — we'll mention first of all appraisal of training. Validation will look at all aspects of the training, including:

- training objectives
- learning objectives
- learner support
- management
- administration
- follow-up.

Validation should also look at the state of the training market — we mentioned the idea of training being a marketable product the same as any other in book 2 of this series *Planning a Training Strategy.* Validation can keep you in tune with the market, by finding out:

- whether the need and the demand for that training are still there
- whether that training is actually satisfying that demand.

You see that the results of a validation could lead you to submitting a request for more trainers and more time to deliver what is a very useful and popular course.

If you're thinking that validation sounds like a large investment of time and resources, then we'd agree. And being thorough pragmatists, we would even recommend you not to validate short, one-off courses, or courses which are perhaps semi-permanent but very small scale. On the other hand, validation is essential for courses which:

- are run regularly over several years
- are used by several departments in large organizations
- are designed for a large and competitive market
- need to have their effectiveness checked by an external professional body.

Remember that most validation is a matter of 'just making sure' or 'just proving the point'. But, since in that unalterable law there is always something that goes wrong, you would do well to leave in your schedules an opportunity to redraft or revise completely some elements of the training being validated.

Formative evaluation is rather a grand phrase for the kind of evaluation experienced trainers are probably all familiar with. It's to do with monitoring the effectiveness of different aspects of training on a continuous basis with a view to modifications. It can be carried out on an informal or a formal basis, or both, but there is one style of informal formative evaluation which is **not** acceptable taken on its own — and it's the one most often used on its own.

Write in this box which style of informal formative evaluation we cannot recommend on its own.

It's the trainer's instinct. It's that feeling that things are going well or badly, and while, taken in conjunction with other styles, it is very useful, and while it may indeed be reliable, some, if not most, of the time, we advise caution because:

- you have invested a lot of time, effort and personality in your training provision, so you can't be sure you're being truly objective.

Use your trainer's nose all the time, but don't rely on it to make decisions. If you get suspicious of a piece of training, then evaluate it formally as well as by instinct. As we said earlier, there are many different techniques you can use, and they're explored in the next chapter. For now, just bear in mind that everyone who is in contact with your training is making at least personal, subjective evaluations about it. Some of them may be making more formal records of progress. One way or another, there are a tremendous amount of data to be had should you need to use them.

Following on from this point, we would also recommend that formative evaluation be carried out on a 'little and often' basis rather than anything else. Formative evaluations which take place every year or so tend to be overwhelmed by the amount of data they generate, and consequently fail to give feedback either quickly or accessibly. Besides which, there are plenty of occasions in the course of a year for a piece of training to go off the rails, so infrequent 'snapshots' of the state of affairs may mean that:

- when you find out about it, it's too late to react
- when you do your evaluation, all you see is that things are failing — and it is sometimes problematic to comb back through previous weeks and months to find out the cause of the failure.

When to Ask Questions (3) — The Final Phase

The final phase of evaluation is called the summative phase, and it should take place at the end of short training events, or as soon as certain discrete sections of written or computer materials have been completed. Every item of training should have a summative evaluation, irrespective of its size.

But what of training that is continuous? That rolls on from year to year? Ideally, summative evaluations should take place at what we call 'natural breaks' — when certain learners reach milestones in their training scheme. Alternatively — and this is particularly useful for training which people can progress through at their own speed and which potentially could take years to complete — you can do summative evaluations at arbitrary intervals, perhaps a year or 18 months, when you can find out what people have learnt over that period of time, how much it has cost, and how much value it represents to the organization.

The summative evaluation fulfils three important purposes:

- it provides a detached, objective appraisal of data
- it provides the data you need to help solve problems and improve the future effectiveness of training
- it identifies a need for training you are not as yet providing.

Detached, objective appraisal

There are many people with an interest in how your training is contributing to the business:

- yourself and your team, who need to know their level of achievement
- your customers — usually the managers who commissioned and paid for the training, who need to know what they've got for their money
- your sponsors — usually senior figures in the hierarchy, who need to know whether the organization as a whole has benefited sufficiently from what you have achieved.

For those people, an evaluation with even a hint of 'trainer's instinct' about it will not be good enough. Similarly, given the choice between a completed evaluation and one whose data are still being generated, they will plump for the former, because it's neater and more reliable.

Finally you should consider yourself in all this, and the way people look at you. When you're asked how much value training has added to the organization, which would you rather reply:

- 'I don't know yet . . . '
- 'It's hard to say at the moment . . . '
- 'That's not the question you should be asking . . . '
- 'Here are the facts and figures for the last 12 months; these here are new courses . . . '

Put like that, you can see the need for summative evaluation on many levels.

Future effectiveness

We have known trainers to regard the summative evaluation as the end of a given piece of training. This can lead to certain mistakes occurring.

Case Study

The management support department of a leading hotel chain sent all five of their desktop publishing staff on a course to learn the intricacies of a new package. They came back from the course apparently well able to cope with the new package. The trainer who evaluated the course asked questions which were specific to that course:

- How long did it last?
- Was it worthwhile?
- Are they better able now to cope/do their jobs?

And the evaluation revealed that the course was a success.

When, two years later, the same people went on an upgrade course, things went less smoothly, and the trainees showed signs of frustration. Why? Because they had decided among themselves after the original course that the learning could have been better if one of them had gone on the course first, picked up the information that was available, brought it back to the office and applied it. Then, when the limitations of the learning became clear, the other three people could go on the course with certain specific objectives in mind — namely, to plug the gaps left by the course. They were hoping to apply this two-tier approach to the upgrade course, but they never got the chance.

The trainer should have asked questions like 'What would you do differently next time?' in his original summative evaluation. This would have given him a more meaningful perspective on the future as well as the past.

Training you're not providing

It is possible that in an evaluation you may come across training which is failing not because of a flaw in its design or construction, but because of some previously undiscovered factor — perhaps lack of opportunity to practise a skill, or the absence of expected management support. This is all vital information for the future planning of your function and of the whole organization.

Summary

In this fourth and crucial chapter of this book, you first of all examined the things you need to look at when you're evaluating training: the impact on job performance, and its impact on the way the organization thinks, feels, acts and reacts.

To measure the impact of training on job performance, you need to ask questions about:

- the improvement measured and observed at the workplace

- the effectiveness of the learning as measured under controlled conditions

    and

- the design of your training.

Reading about how to evaluate the intangible effects which training has on your organization, you saw the difficulties which may stop you carrying out this task accurately, notably:

- the number of variables in any evaluation equation at this level
- the difficulties of setting up a control experiment.

You then saw, however, that it is crucial to evaluate at this level despite these difficulties, and that you can achieve success in these ways:

- by applying the pyramid principle
- by monitoring key events.

You also saw that **only training which impacts on job performance** can go on to affect the organization in a positive, but tangible way.

The second half of the chapter looked at the times and occasions when you should ask your evaluative questions, and to enable you to get a proper focus on the issue, we divided the evaluation process up into three sections:

- the trial phase — which included developmental tests and pilot tests
- the ongoing phase — which included validation and formative evaluation
- the final phase — where you use your data to make an objective appraisal of training's contribution, plan its future effectiveness and identify gaps in your training provision.

Assignment:

Analyse your current training provision in the following way:

1. *Create a matrix like the one below, except with separate items of your training provision listed across the top by name.*

2. *If your training has been successfully evaluated in the ways listed down the left-hand column, then you should score it 1. If it has been unsuccessfully evaluated in that way, score it 0.5. If it has not been evaluated in that way at all, score it 0.*

	Item 1	*Item 2*	*Item 3*	*Item 4*
Developmental Test				
Pilot Test				
Validation				
Formative Evaluation				
Summative Evaluation				

Write down a sentence or so to explain why there are any scores of 0.5 or 0, remembering that not all these evaluation opportunities apply to all items of training. If you can find no valid reason for a less than full score, prepare an action plan to remedy the situation, stating which of these evaluative opportunities you need to address first.

Evaluative Techniques

The evaluative opportunities you've read about in the previous chapter must not be confused with evaluative techniques. Any of the opportunities can be taken using a whole variety of techniques. Even before starting this chapter in earnest, it is clear that the more sophisticated techniques will not be best suited to opportunities like the developmental test, which we've previously categorized as 'rough-and-ready'. By a similar token, the less formal and more intuitive techniques, while they have their part to play, will not on their own be suited to opportunities which require a more objective, formalized result, such as the summative evaluation.

By the time you have finished this chapter, you will be able to:

- describe various evaluative techniques
- describe the circumstances in which each technique might be most appropriate
- match different evaluative techniques to different methods of training
- select and implement different evaluative techniques.

In the course of this chapter we will use as our template the opportunities to evaluate which you've just read about in Chapter 4. At each stage we will suggest methods which could be appropriate and why, and we will highlight any which are particularly appropriate for certain specific training methods.

Developmental Tests — Techniques for Evaluation

Given that developmental tests are supposed to provide quick but rough-and-ready feedback, how would you go about gathering data? Write your ideas in this box.

The techniques we have found most appropriate are as follows:

- informal discussion groups
- personal feedback
- single postal questionnaires.

You should look at each of those in turn.

Informal Discussion Groups

We know of trainers who plump for the 'informal discussion method' for all the wrong reasons, and who consequently get themselves into all kinds of trouble. Informality might sound like an opportunity not to prepare; to wait and see; to let the group have its head and then do a little 'pulling together and summarizing' at the end. Informality sounds like a soft option. It isn't.

The informality of the discussion group relates more to matters of rank, pecking order and opportunity to speak than to anything else. Think about what a formal discussion group would be like; it would probably resemble a debating society, with individuals carefully briefed beforehand and aware of what they were going to say and at what point in the proceedings; there would be programmed opportunities to speak for and against. Or, to take a less straitjacketed example, a formal discussion group would have little opportunity for everyone to comment on everyone else's perceptions. And the trainer is in complete control, but could never be sure that all the ideas were being brought to the surface.

So, informality recommends itself — but what are the dangers of an informal discussion which you — as the 'person in charge' — should be aware of? Write down at least three in this box.

These are the dangers we most often notice on our travels: We've set them out in the grid below, because we're keen for you to say what you would do to mitigate each potentially disastrous situation.

Again, write your suggested actions in the boxes opposite the listed dangers.

Discussions are dominated by a few vocal members	
People are hesitant to express their anxieties in front of others	
Learners have forgotten the factors they're supposed to be commenting on	
Discussions are hard to analyse	

Here are our thoughts on the matter; you'll see that in every case your role as a facilitator is to impose a little formality on the proceedings.

Discussions are dominated by a few vocal members	You should impose new ground rules: insist that everyone has an opportunity to say something in strict rotation, and respond to everybody's comments encouragingly. Tell insistent people they'll have their turn.
People are hesitant to express their anxieties in front of others	Express your own anxieties first and show how it is possible to turn these anxieties into improved training. This demonstrates to everyone that (a) there is no shame in being anxious and (b) revealing the anxieties helps the group.
Learners have forgotten the factors they're supposed to be commenting on	Arrange for the discussion to be held immediately after the learners have trialed the materials; issue joining instructions with a reminder sheet.
Discussions are hard to analyse	Involve the group in the analysis and make notes on a flip-chart; use an agenda, tell the people about the agenda before the discussion, and impose this structure on the meeting. Within the items of the agenda, informality can be given its head. Also, trainers who run **regular** discussion groups become skilled at analysing the discussions.

Arranging discussion groups like this is a quick and effective way of getting feedback, and we recommend you use it, but with two important words of caution.

First, be mindful of who you invite to take part in the trial and, consequently, who you invite to the discussion. It is possible to get sufficient feedback at this stage from the learners themselves, but it is better to invite a manager to observe what is going on and request the manager to add his or her perspective.

Second, even with a structure and strong facilitation from yourself, the discussion will inevitably be a subjective evaluation of your training. Again, that is sometimes enough at this rough-and-ready stage, but we recommend you include at least one objective element in your developmental test.

We have spoken so much about the form of the discussion that we haven't yet mentioned the questions you should ask to get the information you need.

Use the space below to prepare a list of questions you should ask to gain the information you would need to give you the go-ahead to complete the training development, or to realize that you're completely off course.

These are the questions we believe are key:

- What was your experience in this area prior to this training?
- How long did the training take you to complete?
- Did you need any help with the training?
- Has the training helped you do your job or any part of it?
- Was the training interesting?
- Which bits of the training were particularly good/bad?
- Which bits of the training would you change?
- Did you feel out of your depth/patronized?

Get the answers to these questions, add to them a management perspective and you will have all the information you require so that you can decide whether to continue, change or abandon your idea.

Personal Feedback

Another successful method of developmental testing is personal feedback either face-to-face or over the phone. There are advantages and disadvantages to this method as compared to the group method.

The advantages are that the trainer is more in control of the situation and can focus one person's mind more easily than managing the interaction between a group of people. Also, particularly in the case of telephone feedback, the trainer can gather the information at a time that suits him or her. If one of the 'guinea-pigs' happens to be away on holiday or ill, the trainer can always catch up with them later.

The disadvantages are: first, that it can be time-consuming either running round what may be a large building to conduct face-to-face interviews or continually ringing up only to find that the person you need to talk to isn't there. Second, if a trainee knows there's a meeting coming up and that the materials have to be completed by then, they may be more motivated to co-operate than would be the case if they simply expected a phone call; let's face it, it's quite easy to say over the phone, 'I'm sorry, I haven't quite finished yet: can I call you back next week . . . '.

Third, your opinions might be tainted by the reactions of the first people you call on: in a group, two people who react negatively to the training can be seen to be in a minority at an early stage. But if you talk to them one by one, and the first two people just happen to feel negatively about the training, then by the time you call person number three, you could be defensive (not to say shell-shocked!) after what you've just been through.

You can overcome some of these disadvantages simply by being aware of them, preparing in advance and compensating afterwards; so that on the whole, we can recommend the personal feedback method quite strongly. The questions you ask should be the same as those you would ask in a group.

Single Postal Questionnaires

As with the other methods of developmental test, there are advantages and disadvantages to the questionnaire.

The advantages revolve around the fact that there is a higher degree of objectivity. First, the people who fill in the questionnaire are less likely to be influenced by either a positive or a negative group dynamic, and you tend you get a truer impression of what people really think. Second, afterwards, when you are called to account for your decision, you may find it useful to have the completed questionnaires there as proof of the soundness of the basis of your decision. So great are these advantages that we would recommend that even in a group discussion you include a brief questionnaire for people to complete in the light of their discussions.

The disadvantage of a postal questionnaire is quite simply that people tend not to fill them in, in which case you can end up without the information you need and looking less than competent. There are ways to counter this, but you should be aware that, given small numbers, none of these ways is foolproof.

How would you ensure you get the information you require in sufficient quantities from a postal questionnaire? Write at least two suggestions in this box.

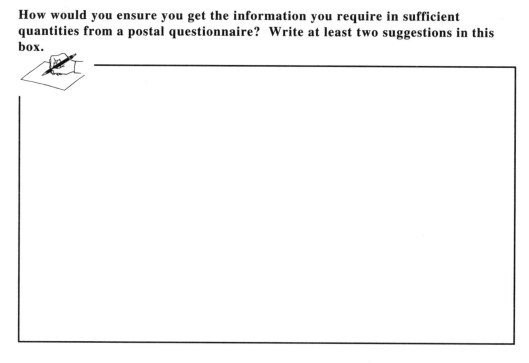

We came up with three suggestions:

- first, ensure that the questionnaire is brief, clear, to the point and well-designed. Questionnaire design is a specific science too detailed to be addressed here, but suffice it for now to say that you must include an explanation of why the completed form is important, and an address to send it to as well as a deadline

- second, offer an incentive to all speedy respondents; we cannot say what is within your gift to offer. Just thanks may be enough

- third, issue an excessive number of questionnaires on the basis that only 50 per cent or so will be returned.

We've gone into some detail about these methods of pilot testing, because, as you'll see, the principles of these evaluative methods will recur at later stages in the evaluation. When they do so, we will allude to them briefly to save going over the same ground in detail twice.

Pilot Testing — Techniques of Evaluation

You saw in chapter four that the pilot test is similar to the developmental test, but goes into greater depth. The methods you can use to evaluate reflect this fact. Without wishing to imply an order of preference, they are:

- questionnaires
- interviews
- behavioural analysis.

You should look at these in turn now.

Questionnaires

Objectivity is crucial in a pilot test, and the only way you can ensure objective responses to questionnaires is to design them in such a way that the respondents' choice of words is limited. In practice, this means including a high proportion of:

- detailed multiple-choice questions

    and
- sentence-completion elements.

So, we would expect to see questions like: 'On a scale of 1 to 10, where 10 is high, how relevant did you find this training?' or: 'Did you find this training tedious/uninteresting/neutral/interesting/fascinating?'.

The questions you ask will be very much as those asked in the developmental test, except that this time you need a greater level of detail. Whereas earlier you needed to know whether the training was useful for the job or not, now you need to know **how** useful it was.

Here is part of the list of questions again. In the space opposite each one write down how you would change the question to make it more suitable for a pilot test.

What was your experience in this area prior to this training?	
How long did it take you to complete?	
Did you need any help with it?	
Has it helped you do your job or any part of it?	
Was it interesting?	
Which bits of it were particularly good/bad?	

Here are our suggestions. Remember that this list is not exhaustive, but it is just an indication of the depth of detail and objectivity you should strive for. Notice that where any value judgement is called for on the part of the respondent, there is some mechanism which restricts the use of subjective or personal language. While this is not entirely foolproof — after all, one person's six out of ten might be another's seven out of ten — it is none the less more objective than mere open questions.

What was your experience in this area prior to this training?	How long have you worked in this area for this organization? For other organizations? (Please list.) What previous training have you had? (Please list.)
How long did it take you to complete?	Did you complete it in one or more sessions? (Please specify.) How many breaks did you have?
Did you need any help with it?	If so, who did you ask? On a scale of 1 to 5, how useful was the help you got?
Has it helped you do your job or any part of it?	Which parts has it helped you with? List them here in order, according to the degree of benefit you got from the training. On a scale of 1 to 10, where 10 is high — how much easier is each part of your job now than before the training?
Was it interesting?	On a scale of 1 to 10, where 10 is fascinating, how interesting was the training?
Which bits of it were particularly good/bad?	List the three elements of this training you most appreciated in order, and the three you least appreciated, likewise in order.

To make your task easier, you can arrange for this questionnaire to be completed in the training offices, so that you have the people in front of you, and you will have no trouble getting a good return rate from your people. If, for reasons relating to the training itself, you prefer to allow respondents to fill them in at the workplace and then send them to you, you must take steps to ensure you get sufficient information back. Some of these we discussed earlier. At this important pilot test stage, you could even 'lean' on people a little by phoning them and reminding them of the urgency of your need.

One final point: we recommend that the questionnaires contain a section where the respondents can say what they like in the way that they like. First, it relieves the feeling of being in a straitjacket which objective questionnaires can give them; and second, you may be able to use any apposite or colourful comments you receive in your report at the end of the evaluation.

In-depth One-to-one Interviews

A pilot test has to be objective, and for the interviewer, that means only one thing: sticking to a script. It's the only way you can ensure consistency. The interviewer may need a thorough brief before he or she launches into the interview, and the responsibility for this brief lies with you, the trainer.

The questions asked should be the same, and couched in the same language, as those on the questionnaire. And, as with the questionnaire, there should be an opportunity at the end for the interviewee to make any extra points, perhaps relating to 'questions they would like to have been asked but weren't'.

Behavioural Analysis

Behaviour is what you do and how you do it, and ultimately all training should result in some form of behavioural change. If you, as a trainer, are to observe behavioural change, then you are going to have to get involved in some very special preparation.

What would you need to have prepared before you felt really comfortable about analysing your trainees' behaviours? Write your answer in this box.

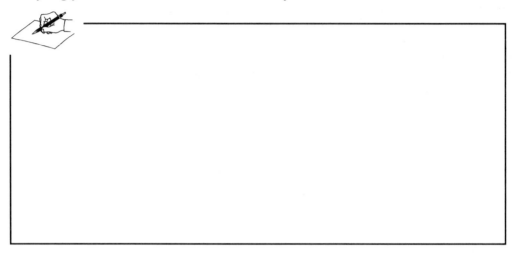

If you are going to do a thorough behavioural analysis you will need:

- a detailed description of each behaviour
- a method of measuring quality of behaviour
- a comprehensive set of checklists.

The detailed description of the behaviour will probably need input from yourself and from a manager or experienced member of staff. You will be able to explain the extent to which the task needs to be divided into sub-tasks, and the experienced practitioner will be able to explain what should be happening in each sub-task.

The method of measuring the quality of behaviour will likewise be a joint venture between yourself and the subject expert. The expert is in a position to say either whether the task is one which permits gradations of success, that is, whether it is a job which can be done badly or well; or whether the task is more appropriately described as a straightforward success or failure operation, with no possible in between stages. You will then be in a position to compose a set of criteria which either match the gradations or (which is easier) a simple pass/fail indicator. These criteria will form the basis of checklists which can then be simply ticked as the trainee is observed.

There is a degree of flexibility about behavioural analysis carried out like this. First, it can be done under controlled conditions in the training environment; in certain cases, such as pilots practising on flight simulators, this is essential. Second, it can be carried out at the workplace as an alternative or as an addition to the analysis in the training environment. If it is carried out as an addition, this will give you very useful feedback indeed — you'll be able to tell how closely your artificial environment mimics the real world.

There is also flexibility in that either you or someone else can carry out the analysis — but on this last point we would add a word of caution. If you choose to involve anyone else in the analysis, make sure that they are properly briefed in ways of observing people. Whereas you realize from your training experience the benefits of adopting a low-profile, non-threatening approach, and the dangers of surprising people with an unexpected assessment, and the chaos that can be caused if you accidentally interfere and tell someone in the middle of an operation what it is they're doing wrong — perhaps line managers in your organization don't realize these dangers. In this case, you'll have to train them in the fundamental dos and don'ts of observing people at the workplace.

Validation Techniques

Validation is that stage of evaluation which takes place as soon as the whole item of training is in place and functioning. As you saw earlier, it's not always appropriate for one-off pieces of training, but for things which are perhaps going to be the mainstay of your training provision for the foreseeable future, it is more than reassuring — it is essential to get it right.

Bearing in mind that validation is the first real check as to whether the whole thing is working effectively or not, what specific items do think it could embrace? Write your answers in this box; you'll see we've left you plenty of space.

We hope you let your imagination run riot with that one. Validation embraces the evaluation of:

- objectives as a reflection of training needs
- administrative reliability and effectiveness
- learner briefing
- the design and effectiveness of the material
- learner support
- individual assessment
- transfer of knowledge, skills and attitudes back to the job
- training records.

This is indeed a tall order, and validation can require as much effort as the setting-up of the event or the materials in the first place. But, as we stress: it's worth it. Think about the alternative — the possibility of that awful dawning realization that something was terribly wrong . . . but you don't know what or where!

No one single evaluative technique is going to deliver information under all those separate headings, and so we expect you to combine the methods we list below in ways which meet your particular needs. Here's the list:

- interviews with sponsoring managers
- administrative checks
- interviews with line managers and staff
- questionnaires
- follow-up checks
- pre- and post-tests
- exercises and observations.

As you read through these, notice especially the slight change in emphasis from that which was present at the pilot test stage.

Interviews with Sponsoring Managers

The sponsors are the ones who empower the line managers to spend their budget on training, and they have a particular interest in seeing that the money is being well spent. While your interviews with these people can be unstructured — we've found that many senior managers bridle at being put through standard questions, and prefer to think that they are in control of the interview — you should ensure that you confirm the:

- sponsors' perception of the current training needs
- behaviours which the sponsors would like to see resulting from the training.

Administrative Checks

The first administrative check is: have you kept a record of what was done throughout the planning, design and delivery stages of training? If not, you're going to find it difficult to check back on what you have done. In our experience the best trainers plan out their training as a project, with each milestone separately entered on a long list of things-to-do. Then as they reach the appropriate stages they can simply tick them off. The evaluation is then straightforward: was each stage done? If not, why not? If late, why late? And if there is a need to change anything, what is to be changed and why?

Interviews with Line Managers and Staff

The interviews you conduct with the staff must have a dual purpose. First, they must lead to an objective appraisal of the training itself. You need to know how long the training took, how much they learnt, how great the impact on the job has been, and all the other questions you asked earlier.

On the same point, you will also be talking to line managers and asking them objective questions about improvements they have noticed in the trainees' knowledge, skills and attitudes; and, as with previous interviews, the questions should be tightly scripted and restrict people's answers using multiple-choice or number-based formats.

Your interviews at this stage must also include one new element which you haven't evaluated at all yet. You may remember from *Implementing Training* that it is crucial to prepare trainees for the training they are going to receive. Otherwise, they will spend valuable learning time figuring out just what they are supposed to be doing there. You must evaluate the degree to which this is a factor in your learning, because, taking the broader view, the feeling of disorientation which follows ineffective preparation for training is a major detractor from learning effectiveness. You want it eradicated if possible.

Issuing effective joining instructions, and engaging line managers in the preparation by sending copies of the joining instructions to them as well as the trainees is a very good practice; and you can help line managers by coaching them in trainee preparation techniques, as we showed in *Implementing Training*.

You must ask questions at this stage to evaluate the success of this strategy. Here are some examples of questions you could ask trainees. Note how objective they are:

- On a scale of 1 to 10, how well do you think you were prepared to take part in this training?

- How long did it take you to settle down into the training routine?

- Were you at any time unclear about what the trainer expected of you? If so, how did you cope?

- Do you know what your line manager expected you to be able to do as a result of your training?

- Have you been able to speak to your line manager about the results of your training?

Questionnaires

Questionnaires at this stage are very detailed and objective. As with interviews (above) there is an opportunity here to sample managers' perceptions in an objective and meaningful way. Below are extracts from validation questionnaires used in a public sector organization which found that its junior people were relying too heavily for too long on their senior colleagues. The organization launched a series of training events under the umbrella title of *Taking Responsibility*. The decision-making element was covered partly by open learning and partly in a workshop.

On the following page you can see what the individual trainees' evaluation questionnaire and the managers' questionnaire looked like. Notice particularly how both sheets focus on what the training was meant to achieve and that both are designed to give consistent feedback.

In both cases, a rubric (not reproduced here) gave the reasons for the evaluation and explained that 0 was low and 5 high.

The Individual Trainees' Questionnaire (extract)

1.	I am more confident about making decisions	0	1	2	3	4	5
2.	I am more confident about the decisions I've made	0	1	2	3	4	5
3.	I give my decisions more thought now	0	1	2	3	4	5
4.	I play a greater part in the decision-making process	0	1	2	3	4	5
5.	I take on more responsibility now	0	1	2	3	4	5

The Managers' Questionnaire (extract)

1.	I can delegate work more confidently	0	1	2	3	4	5
2.	I have more confidence in my team	0	1	2	3	4	5
3.	I have fewer poor decisions to correct	0	1	2	3	4	5
4.	I can spend more time on strategic activities	0	1	2	3	4	5
5.	I have more freedom to act	0	1	2	3	4	5
6.	I have time to break new ground	0	1	2	3	4	5

Follow-up Checks

There is one feature of all effective training that should always be present before, during and after the training event, and your evaluation should check that it is there, and that it is working.

Identify what this feature is and write it in this box.

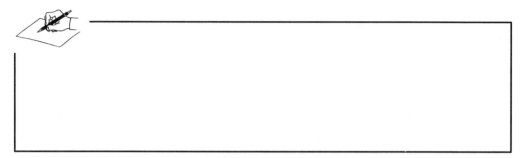

The feature is **learner support in the workplace.**

It could be that you have been providing some of the support, and that the line managers and other colleagues have been providing the rest. Only by asking the trainees and the managers the following questions will you be sure that it's in place and working:

- What support have you given/received?
- Has the level of support been adequate? On a 0-5 scale, how highly would you rate it?
- In what ways do you think support could be improved?
- Would you like to see levels of support increase, remain constant or gradually reduced?

Pre- and Post-testing

This is probably the single most useful evaluation technique if your aim is to measure the amount of change in learners' knowledge, skills or attitudes. It provides a true measure of achievement.

With clear learning objectives, it is fairly simple to set the same or similar questions to test people's knowledge before and after training. Equally, with skills or attitudes which have well-defined opinions or responses, learners could be asked to complete rating scales as a form of pre- and post-training test: the sort of thing where you ask them the thoughts which go through their head when they realize they're going to deal with an irate member of the public. The pre-test might reveal panic; the post-test might reveal greater confidence — an air of 'I know what I'm going to say first and I know at least how to appear conciliatory and non-threatening'.

There is a potential bonus with pre-tests. They help to focus the learners' minds on the key messages of training. We suggest that this will help the learners to pick up new ideas more quickly. Similarly, post-tests will help slower learners to measure the progress they have made.

There is of course a serious danger to be aware of in all this: you could raise the spectre of failure in people's minds. A score of 0 out of 20 in a pre-test followed by 10 out of 20 in a post-test may be statistically wonderful for you, but it could do lasting damage to the trainee. You can only avoid this by being open and honest about your reasons for testing: this means stressing that it is the training which is being measured and not the individual. It can help to make these pre- and post-tests voluntary, so that people will feel like they are helping in an experiment of their own volition, rather than being forced through hoops.

Exercises and Observations

Observation of the trainees at the workplace must be structured, and the evaluation process must record it. Think about what the evaluation is for, and you'll see why. You can't go to the board or a group of senior managers and say that Mr Jenkins in customer services seems to think his new starters are doing fine — so is it all right if your current training budget is increased by 12 per cent? You need proof of improved performance, and that is what a record of structured observation can give you. We've already gone over the basics of behavioural analysis, and there is no need to repeat them here.

You have to be aware of the possibility that certain of the things people have been trained for may never occur, such as fire or serious injury. So in these cases, observation is not appropriate, and you will have to come up with a form of exercise. Provided you ensure that the exercise is assessed according to the training objectives and not according to anything else, you will obtain useful information.

Case Study

A trainer created an assessment exercise in which one of the questions was, 'What is the first thing you would do if you discovered a fire?'. Most candidates answered 'Raise the alarm'. This was precisely the phrase used on the course and the trainer accepted it. One person answered, 'alarm' and was failed, because he hadn't said what he would **do** with the alarm.

It seems to us that this was wrong of the trainer who appeared to be assessing according to the niceties of grammar rather than the training objectives.

Exercises and observation are similar processes from your perspective. There is first planning and preparation, second the actual exercise or observation, third your analysis of the results of what you've seen . . .

What is the fourth and final step? Write your answer in here.

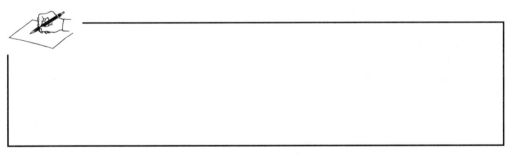

The final step is record-keeping. Both the type of assessment you use and the sorts of records you keep will be unique to your training context, but leaving aside any formal requirements, such as attendance details, etc, it's worth making three points:

- be clear about the exact objectives of any data you decide to keep: why are you keeping them?

- plan your assessment and your record-keeping side by side and at the same time so that you're sure it will do what you need

- beware the bureaucratic storing of endless bits of paper which may be unreadable or impossible to analyse.

This concludes our examination of validation methods, and it is time to press straight on with techniques suitable for formative evaluation.

Formative Evaluative Techniques

These techniques fall under two broad headings: formal and informal. While formal techniques may carry more weight when you're arguing a case with someone, informal techniques have an equally important role to play. Because they are informal, you can use them all the time and be perpetually vigilant; and if your informal techniques indicate something is awry, it is definitely time to apply some formal techniques to confirm your suspicions. This is not to say that formal techniques must only be used as a back-up to informal ones. On the contrary, we recommend that formal evaluative techniques be built into your ongoing training schedule at the earliest stage.

Informal Technique 1 — Instinct

We've just referred to this one; it's where you just feel that things are fine, and you leave them alone, or that there's something wrong and, as a result, you almost automatically change the pace of your work, the activities people are doing or the questions you're asking.

Informal Technique 2 — Observation

Informal observation means looking for signs from the learner that the training is irrelevant or difficult to follow. These signs will mostly be in the form of negative body-language such as yawns and staring out of the window. Also included under this heading are incidents where trainees tell you that a given task is misleading, or that a certain proposition is patently wrong. You will of course take immediate corrective action.

Informal Technique 3 — Questioning

There are occasions in any training experience when it is right and natural for a trainer to ask how things are going — perhaps over a meal or coffee break. If you're not doing this already, make it part of your code straight away; you'll learn a lot about your training!

As you move on now to deal with the formal formative evaluation techniques, we must make it plain that any or all techniques you've been reading about up to now can be used as part of the formative evaluation. It's up to you, but do be careful that you don't over-evaluate. All you need is sufficient information to reassure yourself and your customer that you're doing things right and providing value for money.

The techniques we highlight below are particularly appropriate for formative evaluation, as you'll see.

Formal Technique 1 — Session Review

A session review works on the same principle as a cheese-sampler: to check the soundness of a whole batch, a purchaser will take a sample from one or two individual cheeses and taste it. You need to target individual sessions or individual modules of learning to check that they are sound. The skill lies in choosing the correct sessions to review. Random sampling has a part to play; it can ensure that all those elements of training you perhaps subconsciously would rather not look at do receive scrutiny. But random sampling alone can miss key sessions time and again; therefore you should identify a list of sessions which you have reasons to believe are especially important or particularly good indicators, and set up questionnaires to evaluate them.

Formal Technique 2 — Individual Assessment

What are the benefits of individual assessment — in the form of practical exercises or written tests? Write two answers in the box.

We came up with three main benefits:

- to tell learners how well they are learning
- to confirm that learners are now competent in their new skills
- to find out whether the training is meeting its objectives.

Because these points need to be monitored constantly throughout the training, it is essential that they are built in as a permanent feature from the very beginning.

Formal Technique 3 — Analysis of Performance Records

Don't let the word 'analysis' frighten you here. Without delving into the realms of statistics in a big way, you can ascertain how suitable a given piece of training is for learners from different sub-groups of the population. All you need to do is keep records of the levels of performance pre- and post-training, and then look at these data in the light of the qualification, age and experience of the learners. You will soon see which groups are benefiting most and which least from your training; and then you can adapt your training as necessary.

Formal Technique 4 — Follow-up Visits

Merely visiting your trainees at work isn't going to achieve much. But if you visit them:

- with a wide range of data gleaned from interviews, questionnaires and assessments carried out under training conditions, and

- with a view to confirming and updating that data by further evaluative work with themselves and their managers,

then we believe that a follow-up visit can achieve a lot. Certainly it is essential that you, the trainer, are seen at the workplace, and seen to be finding new and ever-better ways of ensuring that training really does serve the world of work.

Now you're very near the final point of this chapter — summative evaluation. The results of your validation and your formative assessment may be used to make immediate decisions and consequent alterations to your training provision. Or they may be garnered together and used to contribute to the summative evaluation — our next and final point.

Summative Evaluation Techniques

If you have followed the recommended stages of developmental testing, piloting, validation and formative evaluation, the process of summative evaluation need not be too sophisticated. In our experience it is trainers who leave all their evaluation to the end who go through agonies at this stage, because they have to devise tools which are always cumbersome and usually inaccurate to estimate facts which should have been gathered in, processed and acted upon much earlier.

A simple, straightforward summative evaluation has two big advantages: first, you can use it to find out about the effectiveness of the training as a whole, and you don't get bogged down in the detail. Second — and this point is consequent upon the first — you can see how one training element compares to another, which your on-going evaluation can never do.

We suggest the following techniques.

Final Learner Assessment

Increasingly towards the end of training, learners want and need to know:

- what they have learned
- how they have performed
- how they compare with others.

The final assessment can take the form of a test, an exercise or an assignment. This has the double advantage of answering the learners' questions and helping you to measure the success of the training in meeting its objectives.

Group Discussions

We discussed earlier the difficulties of a group discussion and the means of mitigating them. The reason why group discussion is such a useful tool at the summative stage is very simple: it is a natural thing to want to sit down after a new experience and talk about what's happened. Your skill in the summative discussion is to cultivate the relaxed air which should be prevailing while at the same time yourself being far from relaxed; you're after feedback, and you will have to guide learners gently down the paths you want to explore.

Individual Questionnaires

Group discussions can reflect the opinions of a few members. So we recommend that you use questionnaires in conjunction with the group discussion to help to ensure that you get the whole picture — accurately.

'Happy Sheets'

The much maligned end-of-event questionnaires have a lot to offer. First, it may be the learners' only chance to comment on environmental issues, by which we mean things like the beds (on residential courses), the blinds — or lack of them (in conference rooms) and the noise level (if working through a detailed text in a busy office). These factors all impinge directly on the learning and it is worthwhile your knowing about them. There is no point in looking for a design flaw in your training if all that was wrong was some stale sandwiches!

'Happy sheets' also give the learners an opportunity to reflect on whether they enjoyed the training or not; and as enjoyment is such a key motivator, you need to know about it and measure it.

Summary

In this long and fairly detailed chapter you passed through each stage of evaluation, and noted techniques which made suitable evaluation tools at each stage.

Stage 1 was the developmental test where the following were recommended:

- informal discussion groups
- personal feedback
- single postal questionnaires.

Stage 2 was the pilot, where the following more formal techniques were recommended:

- questionnaires
- interviews
- behavioural analysis.

Stage 3 was validation, and this covers so many areas that no one method of evaluation can deal with everything. We suggested that you should choose an appropriate combination from this list:

- interviews with sponsoring managers
- administrative checks
- interviews with line managers and staff
- questionnaires
- follow-up checks
- pre- and post-tests
- exercises and observations.

Stage 4 was formative evaluation, and while we suggested that any of the techniques used in stage 3 would still be worthwhile in this stage, we were none the less able to recommend:

- the informal techniques of instinct, observation and questioning
- the formal techniques of session review, individual assessment, analysis of performance records and follow-up visits.

The fifth and final stage was summative evaluation. Trainers who have followed through the other stages and have made the necessary adjustments to their work as they have been going along, are left with a fairly simple job at the end: to gain information which will enable them to look at the training as a completed whole, using these methods:

- final learner assessment
- group discussions
- individual questionnaires
- 'happy sheets'.

Assignment:

Take two items of your planned training provision and evaluate them using some of the methods outlined in this chapter. Record your progress in the form of file notes, or if more appropriate, using a cassette tape-recorder (as, for example, in a discussion group). Note down (a) why you selected those particular techniques and (b) whether you counted them as a success or not.

Chapter 6

Reacting to Evaluation

This final chapter is only very short, but it has one important point to make which could not logically be dealt with at any other place: what do you do with an evaluation when it is finished?

By the time you've looked at this last chapter, you will be able to:

- say exactly what needs to be done with a finished evaluation
- explain how evaluations lead naturally into the next step up the spiral: the next training needs analysis.

The Finished Evaluation

The evaluation process goes through various stages. Some of these — the developmental test, the pilot, and the validation — have definite end-points within the whole. At these points your only possible reaction is in the form of a decision. Do you:

- leave everything alone, because all the indicators are positive?
- amend the part of your programme which has shown up as being in need of improvement?
- go back to the drawing board?

The formative evaluation has no end-point. It just goes on gathering information allowing you to steer your training throughout its entire period of currency.

The summative evaluation is usually the end-point of the whole training experience. It's too late to change anything for this course, because it is finished. It's too late to go back to the drawing board. There may be a decision to make about whether or not to run the course again next year, or whether to give the next batch of new starters the same open learning course. If so, good. You have the information you need to base that decision on.

But it's possible that the evaluation is complete, the training is complete, and the temptation is to put the whole lot in a drawer and forget about it. Well, don't.

The finished evaluation may need to be included in a report which you will submit to your customers or their sponsors. The time may be several months away, but sooner or later someone will need to know whether that particular course or item of training was indeed value for money. You'll need to have the facts and figures ready.

Even if no one asks, you will need to know from the point of view of managing your own resources whether it represented value for money; and if it didn't, you will be able to design better, more cost-effective programmes in future.

In some ways, evaluations which reveal shortcomings are easier to react to than those which reveal none. In the case of shortcomings, there is an agenda for you to address, there are corrective actions to take, there are discussions to be had and new ideas to be tried out. There may even be a crisis of confidence to cope with.

But what of the evaluation which reveals success? It was cost-effective, it met its objectives, the organization is demonstrably stronger and better able to make its way because of it, so — well done!

Is this the end of the road for your training function? Or is there another message? Write down your thoughts in this box.

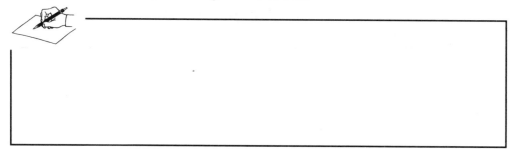

The message is simply this: your training has lifted the organization (or a significant part of it) up a notch so that everyone is on a higher plane. But the people there aren't fully developed yet; there is always some capacity to learn new skills and acquire new knowledge. Consequently, the organization now finds itself able to develop — to achieve new targets in its particular field, or to move out into new fields. There is enormous scope and potential, and if your organization does not seize the opportunity that this presents, it will be left behind — because standards are rising everywhere.

It follows, then, that at a strategic level, those guiding your organization will identify a way forward and upward from the current base. This will inevitably throw up new training needs, and it will be up to you to analyse them.

This, then, is the continuing role of the training function: analyse the needs, design the training, implement the training, evaluate the training, until you know it's hit the target, and then analyse the new needs, all the time raising the standards, the performance and the expectations of the organization and all those who have a vested interest in it.

We wish you every success.

Assignment:

Take the results of your evaluation carried out at the end of Chapter 5 and, in the light of what they reveal:

- *write down what you would do (if anything) to modify or adapt your training provision — and why*
- *write down what you would do (if anything) to modify or adapt individual learning programmes.*

Further Reading

Handbook of Training Evaluation and Measurement Methods
Jack J Phillips Kogan Page 1991

Evaluation: Relating Training to Business Performance
Terence Jackson Kogan Page 1991

Validating Your Training
Tony Newby Kogan Page 1992

Programme Evaluation and Quality
Judith Calder Kogan Page 1993

Measuring Instructional Results
Robert Mager Kogan Page 1991